# Cyberage Politics 101

Popular Politics
& Governance
In America

Steven Schier
*General Editor*

Vol. 2

PETER LANG
New York • Washington, D.C./Baltimore • Bern
Frankfurt am Main • Berlin • Brussels • Vienna • Oxford

Stephen E. Frantzich

# Cyberage Politics 101

## Mobility, Technology, and Democracy

PETER LANG
New York • Washington, D.C./Baltimore • Bern
Frankfurt am Main • Berlin • Brussels • Vienna • Oxford

Library of Congress Cataloging-in-Publication Data

Frantzich, Stephen E.
Cyberage politics 101: mobility, technology, and democracy / Stephen E. Frantzich.
p. cm. — (Popular politics and governance in America; v. 2)
Includes bibliographical references and index.
1. Information society—Political aspects—United States. 2. Information technology—Political aspects—United States. 3. Political participation—United States—Computer network resources. 4. United States—Politics and government—2001- —Computer network resources. I. Title. II. Series.
JK468.A8 F74    306.2'0973—dc21    2002016215
ISBN 0-8204-5246-7
ISSN 1529-241X

Die Deutsche Bibliothek-CIP-Einheitsaufnahme

Frantzich, Stephen E.:
Cyberage politics 101: mobility, technology, and democracy / Stephen E. Frantzich.
–New York; Washington, D.C./Baltimore; Bern;
Frankfurt am Main; Berlin; Brussels; Vienna; Oxford: Lang.
(Popular politics and governance in America; Vol. 2)
ISBN 0-8204-5246-7

Cover design by Joni Holst

© 2002 Peter Lang Publishing, Inc., New York

All rights reserved.
Reprint or reproduction, even partially, in all forms such as microfilm, xerography, microfiche, microcard, and offset strictly prohibited.

# Table of Contents

Acknowledgments..................................................................vii

| | | |
|---|---|---|
| 1 | **The Where, What, How and So What of Politics**......................1 | |
| | The Questioning Life...................................................................1 | |
| 2 | **Where Do You Live?**.................................................................13 | |
| | The Social Shift: From Communities of Total Commitment to Communities of Limited Commitment...............15 | |
| | The Legal Shift: Political Cut-and-Paste.....................................25 | |
| | From All Politics Is Local to All Politics Is Personal................28 | |
| 3 | **What Do You Need To Know? Requisites for Active Citizenship**...........................................................31 | |
| | The Basics: What Do You Need to Know?................................31 | |
| | The Informed Citizen..................................................................41 | |
| 4 | **How Do You Know What You Know? The First Wave of Geography-Superceding Technologies**......................43 | |
| | A Benchmark for Comparison: A Virtually Unmediated Reality......................................................................43 | |
| | Back to the Future: From Hearth and Kin to the Radio Dial.............................................................................46 | |
| | Television Environment: The 800 Pound Gorilla.......................49 | |
| | Fragmentation: The First Shoe Drops.........................................57 | |
| 5 | **How Do You Know What You Know? Computers, the Internet and Beyond**.......................................61 | |
| | The Nature of the New Technologies as Information Providers......................................................................................62 | |

TABLE OF CONTENTS

How You Know Helps Determine What You Know..................92

6 **What Do You Know? The Informed Citizen**..........................93
Who Knows What in the Cyber-Information Age?.....................93
Technology-induced Empowerment?........................................106

7 **The Where, What and How of
Politics in the Cyberdemocracy Age**......................................109
Where You Sit Determines If You Sit: Modern
Political Geography......................................................................109
Information and Political Action: To Know Is to Act................118
Looking out for Yourself: Democracy R Us..............................130
Where Does It All Leave Us?....................................................133

**Notes**............................................................................................135

**Index**............................................................................................153

# Acknowledgments

The origin of this book began when the author was chosen as a Maryland's "Millennium Speaker" by the Maryland Humanities Council and tasked with developing a thought-provoking lecture for the general public. The main ideas were tried out on a number of widely varying audiences throughout Maryland. Their questions helped hone the arguments and raised new questions. Series editor Steven Schier provided careful reading and helpful guidance as did my Naval Academy colleague, Howard Ernst. My wife Jane supplied tough, but honest editorial assistance. Professor Eloise Malone helped unlock key data from the Inter-university Consortium for Political Research. Barbara Breeden of the U.S. Naval Academy Library provided important information sleuthing, while Ken Mierzejewski provided furnished graphics support.

# Chapter 1
# The Where, What, How and So What of Politics

## The Questioning Life

The active life involves a series of questions. Individuals with active minds ask questions about their environment and about themselves. Education (as opposed to training or indoctrination) consists of questioning the facts, assumptions and interpretations provided by others, eventually forming our own set of facts, assumptions and interpretations which serve as the basis for our behavior. The wise individual recognizes that today's "correct" answers may well be tomorrow's myths and misinterpretations. Until September 11, 2001, the vast majority of Americans felt a massive terrorist attack "couldn't happen to us." Today that hope and assumption seems dramatically naive. Wise individuals learn to ask questions to help understand a changing world.

    Education is a constant process of questioning an ever-changing world and our place in it. Wisdom involves knowing when to maintain current outlooks and when to discard them into the ash bins (a rather outdated concept itself) of irrelevance. When we stop questioning, intellectual rigor mortis sets in. To a large degree, we are defined by the questions we ask more than the answers we give. Different disciplines observe and record the same phenomena and tease out widely differing meanings because of the questions they pose. Political scientists ask questions about the source and consequences of power. Sociologists frame inquiries about the impact of groups on individuals. Historians use questions about the past to better understand the present and predict the future. Each set of questions provides a mosaic of answers that help clarify our understanding of the complexities of life.

A number of basic questions define us as individuals in a social setting:

- Where do you live?
- What do you know?
- How do you know it?
- What are you going to do about it?

The answers to the questions satisfy more than curiosity. On the individual level, the first question helps define us as social beings and serves as a precursor to social involvement. The second and third questions define our informational content and route to public awareness–the preconditions of political behavior. The answer to the last question determines the level and nature of our involvement in the political realm. Answers to the questions affect us as individuals and on the aggregate community or societal level have broad implications for the nature of our communities and society. Honest and complete answers to each of these questions have become more complex with changing lifestyles and the introduction of new technology.

We have all asked the above questions or variants thereof. At times they are simply throwaway lines to get a conversation going or fill a void in a faltering conversation. When we first meet someone, almost the first question out of our mouth is, "Where are you from?" Each question can be asked in a non-threatening manner or, with a slight change in emphasis, can become fighting words. There is a big difference between asking each of the above questions with equal emphasis on each word and asking the same questions emphasizing the word "you." Try it an see how threatening it sounds.

While the questions are familiar and may seem quite simple, the answers are much more complex. They reflect some of the most basic aspects of the human condition. The changing nature of the answers affects society in general and its political and governmental components in particular. Politics is the process by which we as a society determine priorities for collective action. Should we build roads or schools, pay off our collective debts or provide more public services, attack an enemy or sit down and negotiate? Government is that organization in society having the legitimate rights and resources to enforce our collective action by marshaling resources and punishing those unwilling to follow the collective decision.

## Where Do You Live?
## From the Founders to the New Frontier

Where one lives determines under which government or governments one must live and in which political processes one has the right and ability to take part. Traditionally, American politics and government have largely been defined in geographic terms.

The Founders were intimately concerned with geographic linkages. They arrived at the Constitutional Convention more to protect their local communities and colonies than to build a nation. Transportation limitations in the large and expanding land meant that few citizens traveled more than a few miles from their communities of birth. Loyalties to towns and counties initially greatly surpassed those to colonies or any larger emerging political identity. Political activists joined the Revolution with a loyalty to their colonies, newly christened as "states," that was largely undiminished by victory. The Articles of Confederation legitimized state power over the distant and seemingly irrelevant national institutions. While the recognition of the need for more national power served as the engine for drawing up a new constitution, state loyalties served as the brakes for determining the delegates' positions on issues and limited the power of national institutions. Battles raged over the benefits granted to states with large populations and those with small populations.

The Constitution that emerged contained a number of significant provisions and encouraged individuals to think in terms of geographic boundaries. The Senate reflected an intentional design to represent the corporate interests of *states*, more as geographic entities than as a convenient way to aggregate individuals. Districts for the House of Representatives followed geographic boundaries of rivers, mountains and lower-level political jurisdictions. The goal lay in linking like-minded individuals to a single representative. The Founders intentionally rejected multi-member districts, allowing the voter to personally define his or her own representative. Although women could not vote, they were seen as being "virtually" represented by elected officials from the geographic districts in which their male friends and relatives were allowed to participate. The Founders also eschewed dividing representatives according to purported policy interests, such as occupation, if such divisions failed to occur along with geography. Requirements for voting or running for office involved legitimacy based on physical residence. Those relatively few citizens who moved did not take their political rights of voting or running for office with them. They were limited to the political involvement allowed in their new geographic location. Individuals moving to geographic locations not yet granted statehood no longer had representatives in Congress.

For most of the initial two centuries of American political history, the cry for states rights was louder and clearer than the cry for individual rights. On a day-to-day basis, our ancestors confronted state and local laws that varied by geography. What was allowed in one jurisdiction was illegal in another. Some of us come from jurisdictions where slaveholding was legally protected and others from areas that served as the hotbed of anti-slavery. What government provided in one jurisdiction was not necessarily provided in another. Some areas of the country quickly provided computers in the schools, while others lagged far behind. The courts largely upheld differences in government services and the enforcement of regulations based on geography as long as all residents *within* a recognized geographic political unit received similar treatment. Protests exclaiming the abrogation of the Fourteenth Amendment's right of "equal protection of the laws" largely fell on deaf ears as long as citizens *within* a geographic boundary were treated equally. Where one stood in politics depended on where one lived.

Even a political activist such as Abraham Lincoln, remembered for his dramatic action to maintain the geographic unity of the country against the attempt to sever the union, argued "that each community, as a State, has the right to do exactly as it pleases with all the concerns within that State the interfere with the right of no other State, and that the general government, upon principle, has no right to interfere with anything other than that general class of things that does not concern the whole."[1]

Individuals themselves largely defined themselves in geographic terms, either where they came from or where they currently lived. Individuals went through life with nicknames like "Tex," "The Virginian" and "Minnesota Fats." Past geographic linkages remained largely symbolic, while current geographic ties affected one's political life more directly. To some degree, length of geographic affiliation served as a surrogate measure of one's reliability, especially on issues affecting one's geographic home. Members of Congress were, and largely still are, "hometown boys" and, more recently, "hometown girls." It is almost impossible to gain a party nomination, much less election to Congress, without having acquired at least two of the three pieces of evidence showing one's local tie: being born in the district, being educated in the district, or establishing a career (preferably long-term) in the district. "Carpetbagger" is the special derogatory term for the individual with the gall to assume that geography no longer counts in politics. The carpetbagger's flimsy container for possessions implies to many the obviously temporary and self-serving intention of using a short-term residency for political benefit. Such a limited commitment to the geographic district makes the person's legitimacy suspect. When Hillary Clinton decided to run for the Senate from New York, a state in which she had never legally claimed as her residence, almost 60% of the national population felt it was inappropriate.[2]

Geographic ties also legitimize citizens as they confront government in non-electoral contexts. Members of Congress (and other elected officials representing geographic districts) largely ignore pleas from those lacking the appropriate geographic credentials. They assume that letters and calls from those outside their geographic district should and can be ignored with impunity. Their approach reflects both a philosophical commitment to geographic ties and the recognition that individuals outside their districts have little sway over their electoral fortunes. The redrawing of political boundaries after each census leads to a mad dash by incumbents and potential candidates to convince their new geographically included constituents that they are "their new best friends."

Geographic loyalties have a long tradition in American politics and society. They are endorsed to the degree that they serve the interests of those involved in the political process. Transportation improvements and lifestyle changes undermine the salience of geography. We all live somewhere, but as we will see in chapter 2, more people live in multiple "somewheres."

Where one lives could be a geographic question requiring little but a street address to answer. In the political realm, the answer becomes more complicated with overlapping political jurisdictions with the same street address located in a state, a county, a city, a mosquito-control district, an economic enterprise zone, a school district, a neighborhood and so on. In another sense, where one lives is more an attitude than a location, reflecting where one spends time or reflecting one's interests and commitments. The more choices people have, the more likely that people living in one physical location will not choose the same attitudinal residence.

For most of U.S. history, geographical identity meant one's *physical* location. To the degree that politics and society operate largely through face-to-face interactions and the exchange of physical goods and documents, the limitations of physical presence lead to a limited number of geographically constrained locations for action. To the degree that new technologies make physical interaction irrelevant, the importance of geography evaporates. Virtual communities (as opposed to geographic ones) emerge from mailing lists or on the Internet lack a geographical street address. The political perspective of a person identifying with a school district is likely to be quite different from someone who "lives" on an Internet chat room.

Where do *you* live? Think for a moment about where you *have* lived and where you *expect* to live. If you are not living in the geographic community of your birth, you have experienced "lifetime mobility" and are different than your friends with undisrupted ties to their geographic home. Think about all the political jurisdictions you have passed through over the last 24 hours. Living is more than existing. It involves participating in meaningful interaction with others. Consider the most meaningful interactions you have had in the last 24 hours and think about the degree to which they were tied to a physical location. If you wake up in one community, go to school or work in another, and shop in another, you are not that atypical. Your daily travels provide linkages to a number of geographic and political entities. If you spent some time "living" on the Internet, your activity linked you to a "virtual community," lacking a geographic presence. If your answers about where you live are confusing and complex, don't worry. You represent the norm, not an aberration. We will come back to these questions later. Be assured that you are not alone if a simple geographic location fails to explain your social and political life.

## What Do You Know and How Do You Know It? From Cracker Barrels to Chat Rooms

What one knows determines the resources one has to anticipate and interpret what is happening in the political process and to evaluate government performance. *How* one knows something affects the timing, content and trust in *what* one knows. The what and how of one's knowledge help distinguish the informed from the clueless in a society. Those who know too little or know it too late are more likely to get in trouble for transgressing societal rules. They also exhibit less likelihood of having a say in collective decisions and are more likely to feel frustrated about their political impotency. It does little good to gather information on alternative candidates *after* the election occurs. Knowledge is a precursor to political behavior. Writing a letter to an elected official *after* a decision has been made allows one to complain, but not to affect the outcome. What one knows about politics and government determines what, if anything, one can and will do about it.

In a democracy, the answers to questions about one's information are particularly important since democracy requires an informed and active citizenry. Without the necessary information about the issues facing society, the options for ameliorating them, the legitimate targets for one's efforts and the process by which one can make one's preferences heard, democratic structures are little more than a charade. In the words of Thomas Jefferson, "If a nation expects to be ignorant and free...it expects what never was and never will be."[3] Or, "Enlighten the people generally, and tyranny and oppressions of body and mind will vanish like evil spirits at the dawn of day."[4]

## What Are You Going to Do about It?
## From Cincinnatus to Mouse Potatoes

Democracy is not a spectator sport. Defining one's residency and gathering information are the precursors of action. To the degree that where one lives either facilitates or diminishes political involvement, it also serves to either denigrate or facilitate democracy. What one knows and how one knows it determine one's awareness of problems for which political action is an option and serve as the basis for planning political strategy. Information-processing routines determine the content and spread of information. A democracy worth its name requires that a relatively large portion of the population shares information about the nature of societal problems (the agenda), the options for improvement (the alternatives), the identity of those who will make the ultimate decisions (the targets), and the effective strategies for influencing those decision-makers (the means). In politics, knowing too little or knowing it too late serve as major impediments to influencing the outcomes.

The classic example of the effective and willing citizen is the Roman general Lucius Qunincticus Cincinnatus, who was said to have laid down his plow and left his small farm in 485 B.C. to serve his country. He then returned to the fields on completion of his civic duty. While there is always a need for individuals who choose political activity as a long-term career, the health of a democracy lies in the actions of individuals who regularly float in and out of political activism—informing themselves, contacting government officials about issues, and supporting favored candidates and causes. To the degree that the non-political aspects of human life overwhelm the political aspects in the battle over time and attention, the health of democracy suffers. It is not really a case that non-participation will immobilize politics, but rather that the void created when some citizens fail to participate will be filled by others whose views and interests may well not reflect those of the non-participants. As Edmund Burke put it, "The only thing necessary for the triumph of evil is for good men to do nothing."[5]

Making a difference in the political process requires motivation and perseverance more than special skills or extraordinary resources. Many changes in American politics have been made by some of the most unlikely activists. Rosa Parks, a mild-mannered seamstress, forever changed the course of civil rights in America by refusing to give up her seat to a White man. Candy Lightner, a political neophyte spurred to action by the death of her daughter at the hands of a drunk driver, spawned an avalanche of state and national laws that changed the drinking age and revised drunk-driving penalties. Gregory Watson, frustrated by a C on a political science paper, quit school and led a movement which resulted in a constitutional amendment. Lois Gibbs led a movement, financed by bake sales, which eventually led to the most extensive and expensive environmental legislation in history.[6] This list goes on, but the lesson remains. Dedicated and persistent individuals serve as the basis for many social and political movements.

To some degree, the geographic basis of American politics makes activism more likely to contemplate since it constrains our area of concern to a manageable set of boundaries. It is like the pragmatic businessman on vacation at the beach. One morning he looked out to see the shoreline littered with thousands of starfish washed up by a high tide. Out of the water, they would surely die. As he contemplated the magnitude of an effective rescue effort, he saw a young boy staking out a few yards of beach in front of his family's beach house and carefully returning the starfish in that area to the water, one at a time. The businessman rushed down to the beach thinking of the immensity of the task and exclaimed to the young boy, "What you are doing isn't making any difference." The boy picked up a starfish, walked to the water, gently dropped it in, and said, "Well, it sure will make a difference to this one."[7] Solving all the problems in politics is well beyond our reach, but we may be able to solve some of the difficulties we observe on our "beach."

## Seeking Answers, Taking Action

Answering the questions about where one lives, what one knows, how one knows it and what one will do about it may seem simple on the surface, but often the seemingly most simple questions require complex and sophisticated answers to reach true understanding. The answer to one of the questions affects answers to the others. Where one lives leads to information-gathering routines relevant to one's physical or attitudinal residence and suggests the types of political activity to which one might reasonably aspire. Most of us know more about politics in our state than that of any other. As we travel around the country, we pick up *USA Today* and make a mad dash to the state-by-state roundup, looking for the headline stories from *our* state.

Information-gathering routines often determine what one knows and when one knows it. The source, content and timing of one's information in turn determine what one can do with that information to understand or affect the political process. Political action is not necessarily the last or concluding step in the process. Individuals goaded into political action before becoming fully informed are often motivated to change their future information-gathering routines to fill in the gaps. Once political action is taken, individuals often develop a new sense of identity with the geographic or attitudinal community in which they took action. Satisfactory political involvement may lead to a deepened commitment to the community, more intensive information gathering and a further round of action. An unpleasant experience may lead to defining oneself out of the community ("If that is the way they want it, let them stew in their own juice") and an information-gathering process that censors information on particular topics or locations.

The answers also become complex because they aim at a moving target. Social and technological changes change options for residency, the timing and content of information, information-gathering capabilities, and the options for taking political action. The answers for our parents or older siblings potentially differ for us or for or our children. A decade ago the terms ".com" or ".org" were merely gibberish and targets of our computer's spell-checker (a new concept in and of itself). Today those terms permeate our conversation, carrying rich connotations like those of "real" words. If you lack the information to speak the contemporary language, you marginalize your potential for involvement in contemporary society.

The premise of this book is that as we begin the new millennium and the third century of the American experiment in representative government, powerful social and technological forces are changing our answers to these questions: Where do you live? What do you know? How do you know that? What are you going to do about it? Our changing answers to these questions will serve as a backdrop to help determine both our individual roles and the changing nature of the American experiment. Just as we have more choices in answering the questions, there are more choices as to how we will structure individual and collective responses to the consequences. Just as the old answers and their consequences were not inevitable, the new answers and their consequences are not set in stone. As social analysts, understanding the questions and assessing the new answers will help us explain the current state of American politics and government and increase our chances for predicting what the future of those dual endeavors might look like. On the individual level, understanding the questions and assessing our own personal answers will allow us the potential to bring our behavior patterns more closely in line with our true interests and to lead a more meaningful life in the changing world into which fate has dropped us.

# Chapter 2
# Where Do You Live?

> Most homelands for Americans are no longer geographical. The Internet community, the journalists' community, the rock-and-roll community, though all homes of a sort, aren't bound into bits of soil. These days when we die, the friends we made over a lifetime don't walk to the funeral. They fly in from all over.
> —Paul Richard, "For Americans, Homeland Is Down the Road a Piece, *Washington Post*, September 22, 2001

On the surface, the question Where do you live? appears mundane—even trite. We have all answered it hundreds of times on forms and in personal conversation. Many of us can rattle off a series of street addresses reflecting our peripatetic past. Even Alzheimer's patients often can remember their address when most other cognitions have faded. Increasingly, though, the answer to this question is complex and conditioned. For "living" is as much a transitory state of mind as a physical reality. The factors that tie us to a particular location have been loosened by modern technology and lifestyles. Over one's lifetime, the permanence of commitment to a particular geographic location has declined as physical mobility has become both easier and more likely to be required by the demands of further education and employment. At any one point in time, modern individuals cross numerous physical borders as they pursue the demands of modern life. At the same time, political boundaries are geographically fixed. Political involvement often requires convincing others (such as voting registrars or simply fellow citizens) of one's legitimate tie to a particular geographic entity and the ability to convince oneself that activism within a particular geographic set of political boundaries is worth one's effort.

Underlying the concern with geography is the undisputed evidence that traditional political involvement has declined significantly over the last half century. Whether one focuses on more clearly political actions (i.e., voting and campaigning) or more indirect measures of community activity (i.e., contacting political officials or joining organizations), Americans have increasingly absented themselves from the community and, particularly, the political playing field. Robert Putnam's evocative title, *Bowling Alone*, sets the stage for his exhaustive empirical analysis of the rapid decline of community involvement this century and generates an extensive national conversation on the decline of civic "capital."[1] He points out that "Declining electoral participation is merely the most visible symptom of a broader disengagement from community life. Like a fever, electoral abstention is even more important as a sign of deeper trouble in the body politic than as a malady itself. It is not just from the voting booth that Americans are increasingly AWOL."[2] Putnam and others go on to point out that reduced participation flies in the face of widely accepted precursors of political involvement. Considerable empirical evidence shows that participation increases with one's level of education, while both logic and data suggest that lowered information costs would make participation more feasible. Despite increased levels of education and the emergence of the information age, participation has continued its decline. In searching for alternative explanations, the impact of geography stands out as one fruitful route.

Political gatekeepers seldom have geography far from their minds. Voter registration is based on one's legal residence. The most common reason given for not registering to vote is the inability to meet local residency requirements.[3] Elected officials largely respond to individuals residing within the geographic boundaries they legally represent. Political information providers in the print media often aggregate information geographically on community pages and/or to geographically targeted editions. Public meetings often require potential participants to indicate their geographic ties as a precursor to involvement. The legitimacy of involvement reflects a "one person, one community" bias. Political officials and other citizens view peripatetic participation as at best unseemly and at worst illegal.

For the potential individual activist, the costs and benefits one must calculate are affected by geography. Local activism is unlikely among those who view their present physical location as transitory. The perception of roots in a community is a precursor to full-blossomed involvement. Partial commitment to a wide range of communities also has the potential for dampening political involvement. The potential activist must first decide to which geographic community to target his or her efforts, and then must struggle to acquire the information needed for involvement.

While both the external and internal constraints on citizen involvement have always been in place, contemporary lifestyles have increased the number and variety of citizens for whom the geographic constraints of traditional politics have become a challenge.

## The Social Shift: From Communities of Total Commitment to Communities of Limited Commitment

> A century ago, social relationships were largely confined to the distance of an easy walk....If one moved from the community, relationships were likely to end. From birth to death one could depend on relatively even-textured social surroundings.—Kenneth J. Gergen, *The Saturated Self*

The concept of "community" implies two related factors. Traditionally, community implied *physical interaction* directly affected by physical proximity. Geography largely determined with whom one interacted. Physical interaction facilitated a *psychological tie* between individuals as they discovered joint interests. Such discovery helped develop a "we" feeling by the individual and a feeling that he or she is "one of us" by others. While geography defined with whom one might develop a "we" feeling, the human dimension added potency to the relationship. Within a geographic area individuals chose those individuals with whom they wanted to be *in community*. Given that choice, geography constrained the options to those in physical proximity. Paradoxically, physical proximity expanded the necessity to at least consider aligning oneself with a broader range of individuals whose only initial appeal was the fact that one could not avoid physically interacting with them. The routines of everyday life led to serendipitous contact with individuals with whom one would not necessarily choose to interact. The town drunk or street person could only be avoided by physically crossing the street. While indifference might develop, it was hard to feign ignorance about the replay of social problems one saw every day. The demand for civic engagement emerged both from one's conscience and from the social pressure of those around one. Not involving oneself in one's physical community was contrary to one's self interest and put one in line for significant social pressure to "carry one's weight."

The more limited the physical ability or necessity to cross physical boundaries, the longer one stayed in a physical community, the longer one anticipated remaining there, the greater the potential psychological tie. Lifelong residents of one political jurisdiction lived in a *community of total commitment,* where the lack of movement across physical boundaries invited a deep psychological tie to the physical community.

As a member of a geographic community of total commitment, the only legitimate way to completely sever one's ties was to physically move —a rather drastic and burdensome option. Over time, physical mobility and the ease of crossing physical boundaries vitiated geographic constraints. Individuals increasingly physically lived in *communities of limited commitment*. Decreased physical interaction with fellow residents and the expectation that today's neighbors would either move or be left behind weakened the human side of community, undermining much of the psychological commitment. Physical communities of total commitment are more likely to develop a feeling that, "We are all in this together. Let's find a way to work it out." Communities of limited commitment invite individuals to pick and choose in which of many potential communities to expend their effort. In many cases, mobility encourages disassociation from all communities where the choice to affiliate is too difficult, the benefits too limited, or the costs of joining quite high.

In the not so distant past, most Americans stayed put over much of their life and lived within the geographic constraints of a limited community. That is increasingly less the case.

## Lifetime Mobility: The Growth of the Peripatetic Polity

Although U.S. history is marked by great migrations, on the individual level most citizens spent the bulk of their life in one community. Traditionally, certain occupations drew individuals to specific communities, while others, such as farming, tied them directly to the land. Even at the beginning of this century, it was common for individuals to be born, educated and married and to raise one's family, begin and complete one's career and die in the same community. Self-interest combined with civic virtue to suggest that political involvement with the goal of improving one's community would personally pay off in later years in the form of increased property values and direct benefits for the individual and his or her descendants. Threats to community life in the form of pollution, lack of zoning or declining services were more likely to be seen as something the citizen would have to live with, rather than something they would likely avoid as they moved to their next area of residence. Living in such a community of total commitment facilitated long-term political involvement.

As two analysts put it, "Citizens who are well established in relationships with co-workers, neighbors, and friends confront fewer barriers to political activism than people who are new to the community. New arrivals face the many demands of relocation....[and] they must reestablish themselves politically....They must wait for new channels to political information and encouragement to develop. They do not yet know anybody, and politicians, political parties, local interest groups, and activists do not yet know them....People who live in one place for many years have more opportunity to develop broader networks of friends and associates."[4]

Residential mobility affects the mobile portions of the citizenry by reducing their motivation, undermining their ability to understand local issues, and reducing their understanding of community norms—all of which work against community-oriented commitments. Even for those who lack residential mobility, the peripatetic movement of their neighbors affects the pool of those with whom they might interact. As one non-mobile individual lamented, "They come and go....We made every possible effort to meet them. But...just when you get to know them they move on...[and] my wife and I are not trained to lose friends every other week, particularly not after we had to work real hard to make them. So we stopped bothering. Now they keep to themselves, and we get about the business of the town."[5]

A simple but empirically unverified mantra of conventional wisdom promulgated in standard textbooks explained declining community commitment with the argument that Americans had simply become more restless over time.[6] If various measures of declining political involvement ran parallel to measures of increasing physical mobility over time, it would be tempting to propose a cause-and-effect relationship. Putnam lays out the appealing assertion that "for people as for plants, frequent repotting disrupts root systems. It takes time for a mobile individual to put down new roots. As a result, residential stability is strongly associated with civic engagement...mobility undermines civic engagement and community-based social capital."[7] Just as Putnam temps us with a reasonable explanation for reduced aggregate involvement in organizations, voting and volunteering, he points out that empirical reality reveals more complexity. During the period of most rapid decline in community involvement the propensity of individuals to move in any one year declined from 20% in the 1950s to 16% in the 1990s.[8] With the proposed causal variable of mobility moving the direction opposite than expected, it seemingly could not explain declines in civic involvement. But Putnam and others may have given up too soon. The overall mobility figures mask two significant caveats. The decline in physical mobility is largely explained by the reduced number of *local* moves. With improved transportation, individuals were less likely to change residence when they changed jobs, trading a longer commute for physical stability.[9] Today over a quarter of the population reports a commute of over 30 minutes to work, with the average length of commute increasing from 21.7 minutes in 1980 to 24.3 minutes in 2000.[10] Commuting time is not evenly distributed throughout the population, with wealthier workers more willing to trade a long commute for the benefits of suburban or exurban (beyond suburban) living.[11]

As we will see in the next section, traversing numerous political jurisdictions creates its own social and political consequences. Local moves disrupt political involvement less since those involved remain in most of the same political jurisdictions. Those moving locally suffer fewer information start-up costs in terms of knowing when and how to insert themselves into the local political community. On the surface, even more distant migration seems to provide no simple clue to reduced political involvement. Between the 1950s and the 1990s, more distant mobility, defined as at least crossing county lines, increased slightly and then declined to almost exactly the same level as the beginning of the period.

While aggregate mobility may have an impact, the question of *who* moves may be even more important. More distant mobility is much more likely among better-educated and more professional citizens, precisely those who have long served as the backbone of local political groups and who are the most consistent practitioners of political involvement. For example, between March 1997 and March 1998, college graduates were almost three times more likely to move out of state or out of the region than those who had not graduated from high school.[12] A similar pattern was not found for presumably less socially and politically disruptive local moves (within a county). Non-high-school graduates were slightly more likely to make a local move. Not only do more of the college-educated citizens move within any one year, but over time many of them are repeat movers. "Average" Americans will make over 11 moves during their lifetime,[13] with the frequency of moving varying significantly with demographic characteristics. Better-educated and wealthier individuals choose to make more long-distance moves, often in pursuit of enhanced job opportunities. Poorer and less-educated individuals choose or are forced to make more local moves as rental agreements expire. Many corporations use the willingness to transfer as a sign of commitment to the organization and as a management tool providing the corporation maximum flexibility in assigning the person with the right skills to the right job without having to concern themselves with personal preferences.

We know from organizations with extreme and inflexible transfer patterns—such as the military—that political involvement is retarded. Despite swearing to "uphold the Constitution" and put their lives on the line to protect American freedoms, members of the military participate in elections at much lower levels than their professional contemporaries in the civilian world. The hassles of voter registration laws and the lack of a physical tie to the community help explain much of the differential.[14]

Physical mobility creates a political brain drain as some of the most capable and likely political activists are snatched from their local community bases. At a minimum the process increases the start-up time necessary to scope out local political concerns and then develop the knowledge and motivation to be involved. At some point, many of these white-collar migrant workers are likely to turn away from political involvement, unwilling to pay the start-up costs yet another time.

Although the problem is not of epidemic proportions, an increasing number of locally elected officials resign before completing their terms. A LEXIS-NEXIS search of newspaper articles for reasons given by local officials for resignation indicates that the majority have been moved by their company and could not justify staying around to complete their part-time, and often unpaid, public position.

Today an "old-timer" in many communities is someone who arrived before you did.

## Daily Mobility: Boundary Hopping for Fun and Profit

> [T]he small, face-to-face community is vanishing into the pages of history... [and] contemporary life is a swirl of social relations....Long weeks in a single community are unusual; a full day within a single neighborhood is becoming rare. We travel casually across town, into the countryside, to neighboring towns, cities, states; one might go thirty miles for coffee and conversation.
> —Kenneth J. Gergen, *The Saturated Self*

In the not so distant past, daily life was more likely encompassed by one geographic community. For many Americans, work, play, shopping and education could all be accomplished within one political jurisdiction. We chuckle at Garrison Keilor's Lake Woebegone lifestyle where people depended on "Jack's Pretty Good Grocery," where "If you couldn't get it at Jack's, you could probably get by without it." In the past, if the local grocery or dry goods store did not have it, one either ordered from the Sears catalog or did without. Customers exhibited a loyalty to local merchants and harbored a suspicion of outsiders. The demand for exotic foods, warehouse prices and the latest brand names was tempered by lack of awareness. National advertising and trend-setting lifestyles of television had not yet emerged. Splendid isolation made small town life more tolerable. In contemporary society, K-Marts, Walmarts and a dozen kinds of chain "marts" put most Americans within easy commuting distance of a nationalized and homogenized set of products and brands. Coupon clippers drive miles to save a few cents, showing no loyalty to particular stores or proprietors (whose names or identities they don't know anyway). Stores, on the other hand, try to lure back repeat buyers with preferred customer cards offering deep discounts "for members only."

Today, most Americans cross geographic and political boundaries with abandon. They live in one bedroom community and drive through a number of others on their way to work in a city or another small town. They do their shopping in a mega- or strip-mall, bypassing the corner grocery, clothing or hardware store in the pursuit of better prices or wider choices. Their children go to larger and larger schools whose service boundaries may have little to do with other political jurisdictions. They travel through a number of political entities in search of recreation or to airports that will take them to even further destinations. Those with children become "soccer moms" (or dads) whose chief role as chauffeur involves driving the beltway or highway, getting their charges from practice to piano lessons and then to a game, often crossing a half dozen state legislative districts.

Participation in politics stems more from a sense of involvement and the potential for identity with a social and political unit. Using extensive poll data to monitor political activity between elections, Sidney Verba and Norman Nie pointed out in the 1960s that " as cities grow in size...and more importantly, as they lose those characteristics of boundedness that distinguish the independent city from the suburb, participation declines. And it does so most strikingly for communal participation, a kind of participation particularly well attuned to deal with the variety of specific problems faced by groups of citizens....The communities that foster participation—the small and relatively independent communities—are becoming rarer and rarer."[15] There is little evidence of any reversal of the decline of community.

The question for a nascent political activist in such a peripatetic polity is Where can or should I insert myself? Am I concerned about putting speed bumps in my community? Do I get involved in the traffic problems associated with my commute? Do I want to improve parking near my office? Do I want to fight for more advanced placement classes at the unified high school? Do I want to make sure the local airport retains a full range of flight options? The questions are endless—they always have been. The biggest difference is that each question involves a different government decision-making institution (or institutions), and each institution is responsible to a different geographic entity. When more of us lived in communities of total commitment, the potential for participatory overlap was much more likely. Each community had its set of activists, and although they may have specialized, they encountered each other on a more regular basis at city council or school board meetings. Realizing that local politics was a continuous game with numerous rounds involving the same players facilitated understanding and compromise. While the vast bulk of citizens were never active on a regular basis, many could be informed and mobilized relatively easily to vote on key issues.

With most citizens having only limited ties to a large number of communities (and their associated, geographically based political institutions), the barriers to long-term, meaningful political participation have increased. Physical distance dampens involvement. I may be very interested in parking near my place of work, but I may not be willing to drive an extra thirty miles to speak my piece at the local city council meeting about new restrictions on parking. Even if I attend, my political legitimacy may be questioned since my legal (and voting) residence makes me ineligible to directly affect the political future of policymakers in a different geographic constituency.

The problem may supercede questions of attitudes. Modern suburbs, which house the most peripatetic of our citizens, are largely devoid of meeting places. Even if a person wanted to interact with his or her neighbors, it would be hard to find a place to go. For most suburban communities the idea of a town square where people sit and talk is little more than a quaint memory. Strip malls spread people out, rather than draw them together. Megamalls like to be seen as towns that include post offices, libraries, dentists, doctors, churches, and even public schools, but they are usually little more than false facades for a real community. The stores that subsidize these new pseudo town squares show their true motivations when there is too much congregating and too little shopping.[16] They are quick to impose curfews on the "mall rats" (a pretty derogatory term for developing citizens) when human interaction seems to come in conflict with economic advancement.

In another example of form following function, modern houses and housing communities reflect a retreat of community-building architecture. The front porch, where the family used to sit during the evening and welcome visiting neighbors, seldom exists. Its replacement, the back deck, allows hiding from social impositions. Even if one wanted to "go visiting," few communities have sidewalks, forcing the potential visitor to put his or her life in danger walking down the street, or to make the visit a big production by driving. Individuals transition from their cocoon-like climate-controlled cars into closed garages opened by garage-door openers and into the sanctity of their security-system-controlled "castles," largely protecting them from a serendipitous conversation with the neighbors. Once they are inside, air conditioning and the lure of television or the computer draw them away from neighbors.

It is not so much that no one will participate, since politics abhors a participatory vacuum. It is more an issue of *who* participates. The more barriers, the less representative the participatory cadre. The more barriers, the more likely it is that participants will include a large percentage of one-shot amateurs drawn into a single battle over an issue that particularly aggravates them. While bringing in fresh ideas and passion, such activists often lack the broad perspective and willingness to compromise necessary for comprehensive solutions to problems.

## Virtual Communities:
## You Don't Have to Be There to Be There

Communications technologies gave the decline-of-community wheel another spin, facilitating the development of *virtual communities*, with no real physical character. Overcoming the geographic constraints, virtual communities could be built around non-geographically associated interests. Along with the benefit of being able to ignore geography came the associated cost that such communities also lacked the reinforcement of physical interaction. Individuals could come and go much more as they pleased without being missed. The possible psychological tie to the community lacked the undergirding facilitated by real social interaction.

Virtual communities also may lack the motivation and/or capability to forge acceptable political compromises. Since they are often composed of individuals with narrow interests and a limited range of information, there is a greater potential for participants to say "either my way or the highway" (albeit the information superhighway). If a virtual community fails to satisfy a participant, relief from frustration is only a click away. Dropping out of the community is as easy as not answering the next e-mail or failing to access the group's Web site. There is no danger the dropout will see a fellow virtual-community member on the street and be asked, "Where have you been? We have missed you." While online interactions can be intense for some, there is no evidence that the intensity of psychological commitment online equals that of face-to-face communities.

## The Legal Shift: Political Cut-and-Paste

Perfectly good values often conflict with each other. A good case could be made for facilitating representation by combining people with similar political interests *or* supporting the principle of "one person, one vote," but both might not be able to be pursued simultaneously. Through much of American history, electoral boundaries were designed to help establish or reinforce *communities of interest*. Those drawing the lines felt that state legislators and/or members of Congress could do a much better job of representing the interests of people with similar political preferences.

Following the census of 1790, each state was given one congressional seat for each 33,000 residents. While it was largely assumed that members of Congress would be chosen from single-member districts, until 1842 that was not required by law and a number of states used multi-member districts or at-large elections. District lines originally coincided with other political jurisdictions (town and county boundaries) and seldom shifted significantly.

Between 1790 and 1911, as state populations grew and new states were added, the number of seats in Congress was simply increased. The only time a state legislature had to redraw districts was when their state gained a seat. Even then, communities of interest played significant roles, often superceding other characteristics such as population equality and compactness. When the size of the House was fixed at 435 in 1911, the possibility of losing a seat increased the number of times a state might be forced to think about redrawing districts, but communities of interest still loomed large. What happened for the national legislature occurred with a vengeance on the state and local level. Districts for state legislatures, county councils and city councils followed existing political jurisdictions and took into account ethnic and occupational enclaves. Some state constitutions even required that certain geographic entities such as counties be guaranteed seats in the legislature. Under such conditions, individuals truly thought of themselves as residents of a particular congressional or state legislative district, an identity that was reinforced by the fact that other geographic identifications (neighborhoods, ward lines) served as the building blocks for larger districts. In many communities, people were known by the ward in which they lived, with each ward having a political and/or ethnic identity. Given such ties, lon- term political alliances based on geography were likely. Individuals had more motivation to get involved since potential allies were readily apparent among their geographic neighbors and the effort required for involvement had a longer-term payoff since there was little likelihood that the political boundaries would be redrawn.

For years, the courts refused to enter the "political thicket" of redistricting (*Colgrove v. Green,* 328 U.S. 549 [1946]), allowing local, and often geographically based, interests to run free in retaining geographic advantages. In many states, rural legislators, secure in their low-population geographically based districts, refused to redraw the lines to benefit the burgeoning urban areas. Their hesitancy to shift power on the state level also carried over when they took on their constitutional role of drawing congressional districts. In 1930 the largest-population congressional district in New York (766,425) was nearly nine times larger than the smallest-population district (90,671). By the time the courts did step in 1962, Michigan had a district, with 802,994 residents, that was 4.5 times larger than the least populous district.[17]

The Supreme Court's series of redistricting rulings in the early 1960s used the Fourteenth Amendment guarantee of "equal protection of the laws" to institute the "one person, one-vote" criteria for legitimate election districts for all offices except the U.S. Senate. The court effectively reversed the priority of criteria they would accept, with population equality *required*, compactness *preferred* and following the lines of community interest little more than *tolerated*. "Drawing the lines with an eye to numbers rather than natural political communities increases the numbers of districts composed of people with nothing in common save residence in the district. District boundaries are even less likely than before to coincide with the local political divisions—cities, counties, state legislative districts—around which parties are organized." [18]

Redistricting based predominantly on population served to cut many individual citizens from their political moorings with the realization that every ten years the disruption was likely to recur. Identification with one's neighborhood might remain, but its short and particularly long-term relevance was likely to be greatly diminished as the new population driven lines began to slice and dice existing geographic, political and psychological boundaries. As Butler and Cain put it, "Allowing constituencies to incorporate natural communities of interest cannot be easily reconciled with the constant adjustment of district lines...[and] redrawing boundaries necessarily moves voters from one district to another, destroying any sense of contact they may have developed with their representative or with constituency-defined activities."[19]

The wheel of political disassociation was given another spin as party and candidate organizations organized around political boundaries and lost much of the ability to motivate individuals based on their traditional geographic identities.

A marriage of convenience between ethnic minority political activists and Republicans on the state and national level after the 1990 census led to a resurgence of the role of communities of interest with initiatives to create majority-minority districts. Minority politicians felt bypassed by White Democratic candidates who rode into office on minority votes, but too seldom allowed minority candidates the opportunity to win. Republican strategists saw the concentration of minority and likely Democratic voters as a way of winning newly "bleached" surrounding districts. The political boundaries drawn for the 1992 election contributed to the process which led to the Republican takeover of the House after the 1994 elections. The 15 new African American districts and 9 new Latino districts worked as the minority-group proponents intended, almost universally sending new minority representatives to Congress. The results in surrounding districts fulfilled the Republican's hopes. As political scientist Charles S. Bullock pointed out, "all districts held by the Democrats in 1991 in which redistricting reduced the black percentage by more than 10 points have now fallen to the Republicans."[20] Challenges by Democrats brought the issue to the courts, with the Supreme Court prohibiting the use of race as the "predominant factor" (*Miller v. Johnson*, 515 U.S. [1995]) and the courts required a number of states to redraw their lines. The upshot of this action was that all but one of the minority members originally elected in a majority-minority district and then forced to run in a redrawn district has won.

The Supreme Court's and the American public's coolness to reasserting communities of interest, at least in terms of race, as a legitimate criterion for drawing district lines does not bode well for other moves to link citizens to the political system based on their biases and/or group-related self-interests.[21] The value of political equality still reigns supreme and in the process helps discourage individuals, keeping them from joining with identifiably and concentrated like-minded fellow citizens to influence government. In the long run, citizens might rise above petty divisions to emerge with a higher level of political aggregation. In the short run, the legal machinations associated with geographic districting serve to make it more difficult to identify likely political allies and thus dampen the political interest of individuals who fear that alliances once built will be torn asunder by the next round of redistricting.

## From All Politics Is Local to All Politics Is Personal

It is more than "bowling alone." Increasingly, social and legal changes have decreased our meaningful social and political contact. In the not so distant past, former House Speaker Thomas P. "Tip" O'Neill asserted that "all politics is local." That might well have been the case, but it is increasingly difficult for many Americans to find a relevant local point of reference. More and more, "all politics is *personal*," not the most healthy situation in a democracy which requires a rich fabric of joint citizen action. We increasingly find ourselves as mobile "islands" of political preferences. Social and technological change thwarts us from connecting together for greater influence. Our peripatetic lifestyles and our political structure make political involvement a moving target against which we often choose not to exert our influence. No one intentionally planned this decline in political community in an effort to reach their own political goals, but that makes the situation no less real. The situation is not totally bleak, some groups and individuals rise above the impediments. Long-term technological shifts, some of which we will discuss in the next two chapters, show some promise of improving the situation. But, at least for the moment, we must conclude that the answer to the question Where do you live? has become more difficult to answer and more irrelevant to politics.

The average peripatetic citizen is caught in a political time warp. Much of the right to participate still depends on geographic location. On the other hand, geography means much less as a stimulant for association and/or as a spur to activism. It is not realistic to assume that individuals drained of their geographic consciousness will "rediscover" it in order to involve themselves politically. Since politics is low on most individual's radar screens, adding an additional set of impediments is likely to contribute to its disappearance.

Social, economic and legal factors have increasingly torn American citizens away from their geographic moorings setting them adrift from the geographic entities which once served to motivate democratic citizenship.

# Chapter 3
# What Do You Need to Know?
# Requisites for Active Citizenship

> We are captives of the information we know and victims of the information we do not know.
> —Anonymous

The oft misstated assertion that "information is power" is correct in its focus, if wrong in its literal meaning. Information is a critical power *resource*, which can be marshaled by those willing and able to change the course of other's actions. In politics, *power* is the ability of one political actor to change the behavior of another actor, getting him or her to do what the power holder intended.

Understanding the role of information in the calculation and operation of power requires casting our basic questions in a somewhat different form and discussing them in a different temporal order. *What* one knows depends to a large degree on *how* one knows it. Prior to assessing what one knows and how one knows it, it is necessary to establish a benchmark as to what one *needs* to know to take part in a democracy.

## The Basics: What Do You Need to Know?

Meaningful political involvement on the individual level requires information about the following:

- **Political Agenda**: a knowledge and selection of salient issues toward whose solution political action might be applied
- **Options**: an understanding of the proposed alternative public policy solutions
- **Preferences**: a determination of one's personal preference among the options

- **Targets**: an understanding of by whom and when the critical policy decisions will be made
- **Strategies:** a recognition of the needs of the target(s), the resources of the activists and how the resources might be used to gain one's preference

## The Political Agenda

Politics begins with the recognition of a problem one seeks to ameliorate. Not all the frustrations of human life generate problems worthy of legitimate political action. Politics by and large deals with problems that have a significant impact on a relatively large number of people and that are amenable to solution by the application of public policies in the form of laws. The potential agenda of problems seen as legitimate is broad and diverse, while only a relatively few problems garner the public visibility and support to be seen as worthy of individual and eventually collective action. A problem is a variation from what we as citizens see as the desirable state of affairs.

We each begin with a set of values as to what the good life and good society should look like. Within that ideal there is a level of tolerance whose threshold must be surpassed before we become offended enough to act. We may prefer a world in which no innocent people are ever harmed, but we would usually not be spurred to action by a few cases of irresponsible drivers killing innocent children—unless, of course, that child is our own. Even in that life-changing situation, thousands of children were killed by drunk drivers before Candy Lightner rose above her private grief and decided to take political action to form Mothers Against Drunk Drivers, effectively putting a new issue on the political agenda and eventually changing the course of public policy.[1] The discovery of one's stake in a new or existing problem serves as a stimulus to political action.

Not all problems are alike. They tend to fall into two categories, *absolute* and *relative*.

**Absolute Problems.** Absolute problems are situations that so offend our sense of the good society and the good life that *virtually everyone* agrees that a problem exists. Immediately following the bombing of the World Trade Center and the Pentagon there was virtual unanimous consensus that a problem existed and that it was worthy of government action. No reasonable person would conclude that such an event represented how the world should be and that the death of so many innocent victims was simply the acceptable price of doing business in the modern world. Even the terrorists themselves would argue that this was not the kind of world in which they wanted to live but that they were forced to take such action because of perceived evils which greatly offended their sensibilities. Few societal problems are so dramatic and garner such universal acceptance. The issue for an absolute problem is no longer *whether* action should be taken but rather is shifted immediately to a consideration of *which* actions are preferable. In the post–September 11 world, expanded funding for airport security and a commitment to destroy the terrorist networks became goals of virtually every American. The battle became one of how to accomplish the amelioration of a universally accepted set of problems. Only a handful of problems garner wide enough acceptance to fall into the absolute category.

**Relative Problems.** Relative problems require surpassing a lower threshold of determination and public support. Many problems enter the agenda by having the ability to convince *some well-placed* citizens that their existence offends them enough to warrant action. The justification for a relative problem may follow a number of courses. Proponents might argue that *relative to other problems in society*, the one they propose for the agenda is more important. Recurring public policy battles over "guns versus butter" pit two widely accepted societal goals, national defense and domestic well-being, with the relevant issue of how to divide scarce societal resources.

Asserting that a problem deserves a place on the public agenda, proponents might argue that *relative to the functioning of society in the past*, things have become worse, so public action is legitimate (i.e., gun-control became an issue as over time more and more innocent victims were killed by guns).

Alternatively, proponents of including an issue on the policy agenda might argue that something is a problem when our society is doing worse on an issue *relative to other political entities against which we like to compare ourselves* (i.e., gun-control proponents like to point out the number of gun deaths in the U.S. compared to those in other Western democracies).

**Controlling the Agenda.** Focusing public and policymaker attention on a problem is a first step toward stimulating government action. Placing something on the political agenda does not necessarily define *what* should be done, only that *something* needs to be changed. Understanding how items enter the consciousness of individuals and get on the public agenda is a critical component of what we know politically. Neither individuals nor policymakers can consider taking action on a problem until they have an awareness that a problem exists. As we consider the process and content of informing citizens in the next two chapters, it will be important to determine the changing ways in which awareness develops.

**Recognizing the Options and Choosing One's Preferences**

Once a problem is defined, the potential citizen activist needs to know the options for solution and which ones he or she prefers. Potential solutions are evaluated both in terms of their predicted effectiveness and in light of how they impact other preferred outcomes. Not all good outcomes are consistent with each other. We each carry within our set of goals multiple values we desire society to pursue. I may want to reduce gun violence, but I don't want to completely give up my freedom to protect myself by enacting a ban on all guns. I may prefer reducing the national debt, but not at the expense of increasing my taxes and undermining my level of financial comfort.

We face policy decisions by recalling past experiences, applying analogies and/or using conceptual shortcuts. The experiences or analogies may stem from our own backgrounds or may be borrowed from others as transmitted directly from individuals or collectively by the media. Around many issues there develops a collective conventional wisdom which defines the appropriate analogies and undergirds them with experiential references. Contemporary Americans would be hesitant to endorse military involvement if they accepted the projection that it was likely to be "another Viet Nam." Government funding for research would likely be supported to the degree an individual accepted the assertion, "American ingenuity eradicated polio, we can do the same with cancer."

Alternative packages of accepted conventional wisdom develop in the form of partisan and/or ideological preferences. Partisans come to believe that taking the position of their party or their ideology is the most likely way to reach the desired ends. Undergirding partisan choices and also existing separately are ideologies which represent both different goals for society and different assumptions about how to reach those goals. Individuals accepting alternative ideologies simply see the political world in a different way. For example, one of the factors that divides most liberals and conservatives is a definition of the primary role of government. Liberals see the ultimate goal as protecting *freedom*, while conservatives see it as preserving *order*. Thus, when it comes to extreme cases of political expression, liberals would allow such things as burning the American flag as an expression of freedom, while conservatives see such an act as undermining societal order.

Partisan preferences and ideological outlooks are learned perspectives on the world determined by the information individuals receive and the interpretive tools they accept. Any bias in one's information gathering or in the rules one uses to accept or reject information is likely to reinforce one's partisan and/or ideological outlooks.

## Choosing Targets and Determining Strategies

Having a preference amounts to little if one does not know where to direct it and how to increase the potential impact of one's action. Political power involves changing the behavior of *relevant* individuals in the direction intended by the power wielder. In a democracy the relevant targets and acceptable strategies are varied. Talking to one's friends and neighbors in the hopes of affecting their votes or encouraging them to write letters to the appropriate decision-makers are both appropriate and potentially effective. Choosing the appropriate decision-makers is complex in a federal system with separation of powers. The responsibilities for making decisions are often clearly defined, and misdirected appeals face the danger of being lost. Writing one's member of Congress about potholes in one's street is as misguided as asking a local government official to change U.S. foreign policy.

The effective citizen needs to know what decisions are in the offing, when those decisions are likely to be made and who will be making them. Once the target and timing have been determined, the next step is to determine which strategies are available. Strategies vary depending on the nature of the issue, the timing and the target. What might work to move the local city council would be unlikely to work (and perhaps even be illegal) when trying to get a favorable ruling by the Supreme Court. In a democracy, numbers count in elections and when expressing one's opinion. In order to marshal numbers of citizens, effective communications tools must be available. The nature of the communications networks in a society determines to a large degree who and how individuals can be activated.

## Participating in the Political Conversation

> Politics is, at its core, a social activity....In order to engage in politics, people must communicate with others.—Kevin A. Hill and John E. Hughes, *Cyberpolitics: Citizen Activism in the Age of the Internet*

**Initiating Conversations.** Shared content provides the fodder for initiating lunchtime table talk, water cooler conversations, or dinner party dialogues. Social interactions are often begun with the lure of a line like, "Did you see that story on the news last night about...? " The facilitating response allowing a monologue to mature into a dialogue begins with a follow-up line something like, "I sure did, and I believe...." If the follow-up line is, "No, I was surfing the Web last night and did not get to see the news," the potentially engaging line inviting a conversation hangs in midair still-born. Unless there is some shared information on which to build, the dialogue turns into a monologue pretty quickly. The extreme case of missing shared information occurs when two people speaking different languages and lacking the knowledge of any other are thrown together and expected to communicate. They either end up parting in frustration or attempt to discover overlapping meanings in hand signals and/or facial gestures.

Just as too little overlap in information and understanding makes it difficult to launch a conversation, too much overlap kills its utility. Dialogues do not require total overlap in information—and in fact become pretty boring when there is. Just like the two fishing buddies who know all of each other's jokes and decide to number them, just calling out the number in order to save time, most of us would be pretty bored with a "conversation" in which someone yells "number seventeen," and participants are expected to react with a deep belly laugh.

**Islands of Shared Understanding.** Most conversations involve discovering overlapping understandings. In the typical conversation, one participant begins in a somewhat new direction, and then someone else discovers a related theme imbedded in the initial comments. They jump in with their comment and redirect the conversation once again. As we will see in the next chapter, the islands of shared understanding from which we launch and relaunch conversations are more and more difficult to find as narrowcasting of information provides fewer and fewer simultaneous learning experiences.

Effective conversations can be viewed from the mathematical perspective of set theory. Each individual comes to the conversation with a body of knowledge and opinions, some of it unique and some that overlaps with the other participants. The unique material, often in the form of personal stories or experiences, serves as the participant's creative contribution to the conversation, but it is the overlapping knowledge that serves as the glue that ties the segments together and as the launching point allowing the injection of personal amplifications. At a minimum, shared knowledge provides a basis for determining whether one's personal story or unique information is legitimate to introduce at any one particular point in time. During most conversations potential participants go through a multi-tasking process of paying partial attention to the speaker while scanning their human "hard drive" (memory) seeking stories or examples that might apply. Attention to the speaker is important to determine whether a dredged-up story is still appropriate for insertion and to assure that no one else has stolen one's thunder by telling the same story or providing identical information. Timing is critical. We have all been in situations where someone who had not been paying attention inserts what they think is a new idea, only to be shot down by the curt comment, "That is what I just said." In a fast-paced conversation, potential participants store up potential insertions, attempting to insert them when the speaker takes a breath. In many cases, it is a game of one-upmanship, with the new speaker making a comment like, "That's bad, but you should hear about my experience with the department of motor vehicles."

Most potential participants arrive at a conversation with a set of multi-purpose, scripted and well-honed stories usable in a variety of potential conversations. Most of us have our "government inefficiency," "having rubbed shoulders with the famous personality," "been there, done that," and a myriad of other set pieces which have been met with favorable reactions in the past. Potential participants lie in wait for collective agreement on a conversation topic, ready to pounce on it with their example. As long as the most vocal in the conversation agree that the story or information is appropriate, the participant is allowed to continue, either until finished or until another participant is clever enough to discover a word or concept on which to hang his or her contribution. If the insertion is well received, it gets tagged in our memory bank as one worth repeating in a future conversation. Our good friends and associates (let alone our long-suffering spouses and family) have heard our stories dozens of times and either listen in silence or serve as critics (hopefully in private), pointing out, "That story has really changed since you first began telling it." When conversations become completely predictable, they lose most of their value to all participants.

John L. Locke argues that urbanization has decreased the amount of information overlap that facilitates conversation. In small, isolated communities there was so much interaction with the same people that they "didn't need to issue a lot of formal news-laden statements. Their associates usually knew many of the same things...[and] conversations...dealt less often with novel facts than personal emotions."[2] Today in modern urban society the same individuals interact less frequently and in less depth. Conversations often must start with imparting new information to which the recipients may or may not react. If they have the necessary corollary information to put the new information in context and to link it to a further body of information or emotion which they wish to share, the conversation goes on.

**Social Reinforcement.** Overlapping information can strengthen the potency of a multi-person conversation by creating a verbal or body-language "chorus," backing up and verifying the contributions of one participant. Non-substantive comments, like "Ain't it the truth," and nodding one's head urge the speaker on and give the comments validity in the eyes of others. The tradition in some churches of loud "amens," or "Right on, brother," is an example of an escalation of verification that spurs a speaker on and increases the potential potency of the message for others. At political events, cheers or applause serve the same purpose as the speaker hits a responsive chord verifying existing information, presenting it in a new or creative way and/or expanding on it and providing a new, shared basis for further conversation.

**Finding an Audience.** A critical capability in politics is finding an audience in order to communicate with them and hopefully to move them to action. In politics, as in life, we spend much of our time "municating." Before you rush to your dictionary because you and I don't have a shared understanding of that term, let me admit I made it up. "Municating" is communicating without the "co." It involves broadcasting a message without having it received by an audience. It is one step backward from a monologue—a one-way message that is at least received, but not responded to verbally. The municated message is never received, so there can be no response to it.

Creating an environment of enough information overlap to facilitate communication while avoiding the deadening situation of overlap overkill is only partially under the control of the communicator. If the potential audience lacks the basic information to interpret new information or if they lack any interest in the topic, drawing them into the conversation is almost impossible. While a political activist may need to spend some time bringing people up to speed on the information they need to understand the rest of the conversation, too much emphasis on this may well turn off one's audience before the intended "meat" is presented. The less informed will not stick it out unless they find some ideas early on which resonate with their current reservoir of information and interest, while the more informed may tune out due to boredom. Some politicians end up with labels like "policy wonks," implying they bore their audience to tears before (or without) grabbing their attention. Clever politicians know how to meet their audience where they are, and then move them to higher levels of knowledge and commitment about the issues on which they wish to build a political strategy. As the audience becomes more diverse in its information base, discovering where people *are* in terms of information becomes a more difficult task.

## The Informed Citizen

Politics is not a game for the lazy and unmotivated. The rights of participation come necessarily yoked with the responsibilities of becoming informed. What one knows is to some degree determined by what one wants to know, but it is also deeply affected by what there is available to know. As we will discuss in the next chapter, the process of knowing in modern society is in constant flux, with the pace and nature of change particularly dramatic in recent years.

# Chapter 4
# How Do You Know What You Know? The First Wave of Geography-Superceding Technologies

> Technologies come loaded with both intended and unintended social, political and economic leanings. Every tool provides its users with a particular manner of seeing the world and specific ways of interacting with others.
> —John M. Locke, *The De-Voicing of Society*

> Information technology is a malleable tool whose ultimate social meaning, content and consequences are highly subject to the influence of specific political values and interests that inform its use.
> —Kenneth Lauden, *Computers and Bureaucratic Reform*

## A Benchmark for Comparison:
## A Virtually Unmediated Reality

Benchmarks are surveyors' points of reference designed to mark an ideal point from which all measurements and comparisons are made. Most societal benchmarks are learned via rote memory, thereby lacking the emotional component that sears them into our being. The terrorists' attacks of September 11, 2001, caused Americans to recall an earlier era when the bulk of citizens learned about an event almost simultaneously, receiving nearly identical information no matter which news source they chose. Most American adults have now lived through the kind of benchmark experience that seemed to be a thing of the past.

For a number of decades, the news audience has both shrunk in terms of interest and fragmented in terms of usage patterns. Long gone was the era when what we knew was largely limited to what we heard face-to-face from friends and neighbors. Gone even seemed to be the days when a limited number of news outlets portrayed events by presenting virtually the same content. Americans over 50 by the year 2001 only had to exchange a salute to bring back a wellspring of memories of John-John Kennedy saluting his father's casket. All three television networks—the only real-time news media game in town in 1963—allowed the vast majority of Americans to share that moment simultaneously. Newspapers the next day reinforced our collective memory with still pictures. John-John's salute became one of many events seared into our memories by the true mass media era of the 1960s and 1970s. Events such as Reverend Martin Luther King's "I Have a Dream" speech and later assassination, Bobby Kennedy's assassination, Richard Nixon's resignation and the hostage takeover in Iran imprinted shared images on people's minds and assured they would remember where they were when they first heard the news

Despite a flood of other potentially shared national experiences, the 1980s and 1990s had fewer events with virtually identical substance shared in real time. The assassination attempt on President Reagan, the Challenger disaster, the fall of the Berlin Wall, the San Francisco earthquake and the slow-speed chase of O. J. Simpson garnered significant attention, but the audiences were increasingly spread among a growing set of media sources, each of which covered the story in its own particular way. Events such as the Challenger disaster and the Reagan assassination attempt had more collective meaning since the options for presenting the event as a visual were more limited. We saw the same explosion and the same few moments of post-gunshot confusion over and over no matter which media outlet we used. For the other stories and dozens with equal importance, the richness that the media alternatives provided limited the *shared* experience. The growth of cable television and later the Internet created a variegated bouquet of sources, with most individuals only experiencing one or two of the "flowers." Most information consumers were incapable of seeing the broad bouquet or having any assurance that friends and neighbors would have experienced the same set of blooms. The richness of options, individualistically chosen by the recipient flipping through TV channels, selecting which newspaper and which article to read, and/or clicking through the Internet following a highly personalized path, undermined the potential for the shared focus and information necessary for conversation.

With the trend lines indicating greater and greater diversity in media options and audience utilization patterns, the clear prediction was that Americans would have fewer and fewer topics for which there would be enough overlap in interest and information to carry out a civic conversation. The events of September 11 proved to be the exception that proves the rule. The enormity of the event, the nature of the news story and structural factors in news gathering all combined to give young people a taste of "what it was like back then" and to remind others of previous community-building news stories. The enormity of the event led the news media to throw standard operating procedures out the window. The economic bases of the media became secondary as the decision was made to provide coverage without commercials for more than two days. The competitive drive of the media to build audiences by providing exclusives (which by definition are unique bodies of information) was tempered as all outlets shared video with impunity.[1] The location of the attacks and the location of camera crews facilitated immediate and dramatic visual coverage. The visual symbolism of direct attacks on icons of American economic and military strength created searing shared images for the vast majority of Americans (as well as fellow citizens throughout the world). Once our attention was drawn to the results of the first airliner crashing into the World Trade Center, many viewers had the unique experience of seeing the second crash in real time, bringing personal experience to Marshall McLuhan's insightful, but hard to grasp idea that can be paraphrased as "instant information creates involvement."[2] On the heels of the first two sets of dramatic visuals, the enormity of the plot was reinforced by dramatic visuals of the plane that sliced through the Pentagon. In an almost unbelievable overload of shared information, viewers watched in real time as the first and then the second tower of the World Trade Center collapsed with a barrage of falling bodies and panicked pedestrians.

The day was an avalanche of shared experiences, reinforced hour after hour with repetition of the same few images. Many of the distractions were eliminated. The Home Shopping channel closed down for the day. Sport teams cancelled play. The networks postponed the launch of their new seasons. Even the person who might have wanted to avoid being drawn into the shared national consciousness would have to take great efforts to avoid the news. The technologies were harnessed to increase shared experiences.

The results were impressive. Individuals struck up conversations with complete strangers in grocery lines and at gas stations. The opening line "Where were you when you first heard?" echoed among friends and tangential acquaintances. Shared information and shared experiences facilitated shared reaction. The experience would not be forgotten, but the change in information dissemination and gathering would be temporary. Within a few days television networks began talking about exclusives and the comforting if distracting commercials returned, implying a sense of normalcy. Internet news gatherers, who had abandoned the net or at least augmented it with real-time television, returned to their Web sites for information gathering and their chat rooms to express their feelings. The brief moment of shared national consciousness was replaced by a return to fragmented sources and differentially informed groups of citizens. We would never be *quite* the same, but we would largely return to the fragmented information gatherers we had become by September 10, 2001.

## Back to the Future:
## From Hearth and Kin to the Radio Dial

Despite the dramatic experience of September 11, 2001, it is an unrealistic benchmark rather than a prediction of the future. The social, organizational and technological trends are well-established patterns with little evidence of reversal or redirection.

In the early years of the Republic, geographic barriers, audience capabilities and technological constraints meant that information flowed slowly and irregularly. The question "What's new?" was posed face-to-face to neighbors and friends and largely concerned local conditions. A political dialogue on state or national issues was limited to the small portion of the population who could read and had access to a newspaper.[3] Information was passed on to their friends over the back fence or the cracker barrel in the general store. Those instituting the "two-step flow" of information with their neighbors were likely to put their own partisan or economic spin on it. The newspapers were intentionally partisan and the well-informed individual was one who read the newspaper that promoted his (and, less likely, her) partisan view of the world. News arrived in bits and spurts, often long after the event (see figure 4.1).

Effective politicians of any era recognize that "participating in the newest communications technologies becomes compulsory if you want to remain part of the culture."[4] They also know that one does not seek a technology per se, but uses it to gain an audience. Hamilton, Madison and Jay used the technology of their day to write the most famous letters to the editor, *The Federalist Papers*, to newspapers in New York. Their targets were New York legislators who both read newspapers and would be voting on the new constitution.

Technological inventions such as the telegraph increased the speed of information transfer, while social changes such as increased literacy and working for cash created a broader audience for newspapers. The partisan press largely gave way to the penny press, which attempted to expand readership and serve as a vehicle for advertising as a way to subsidize delivering the news.

The concept of the media as an inter*media*ry—standing between reality and the reading public by making editorial choices—became clear. Some semblance of choice remained since most larger communities were able to support competing newspapers, often covering differing stories and taking different editorial positions on issues. The creation of national and international news services and the growth of newspaper chains expanded the news reach of local papers and led to more common coverage.

### Figure 4.1. The Increasing Speed of Media Coverage of International Events, 1776–2001

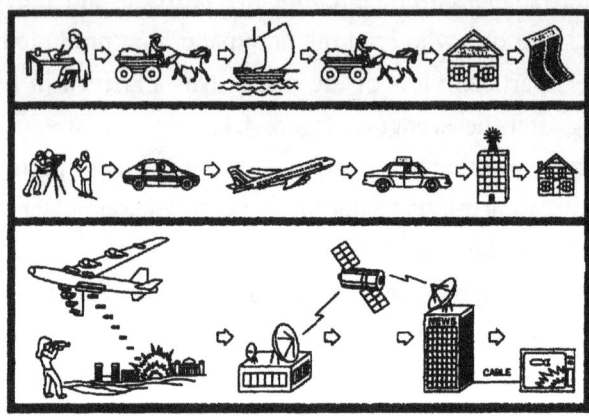

1776  Correspondent travels by horse and ship to report on the king's reaction to the Declaration of Independence. Time delay: 50 days

1815  Treaty of Ghent leaves London on 2 January 1815 by boat and arrives in New York on 11 February. The treaty travels by post rider to Boston, which takes 32 hours. Word arrives that day that Andrew Jackson has been fighting the Battle of New Orleans since 8 January, not knowing the peace treaty had been signed. Time delay: 41 days.

1950  Reporters covering the Korean War send film by plane to New York for broadcast. Time delay: 24 hours

1968  Reporters covering the Viet Nam War send video tape by land to Saigon which is then transmitted to New York for broadcast.. Time delay 12 hours

2001  Reporters in the field use video phones and satellite uplinks to send real-time reports of bombing in Afghanistan. Time delay: Seconds

The introduction of radio increased timeliness dramatically, allowing for virtual real-time coverage of events, at least within the limits of its local broadcast area. The initial local focus of radio shifted to more national information as local stations became part of national networks providing programming. Despite optimistic predictions that radio would revitalize democracy by educating citizens and increasing participation, students of radio history point out that in the drive for larger audiences and increased revenue, radio avoided controversy and provided bland middle-of-the-road programming which tended to reinforce dominant political and cultural viewpoints. Women on radio played traditional roles. Members of minority groups were either ignored or stereotyped. While providing a new vehicle for mainstream politicians to communicate with the public, radio was coopted by existing power holders to pursue their interests.[5]

## Television Environment: The 800 Pound Gorilla

Television aggressively entered the political environment, threatening the audiences of existing media technologies. Just as radio had been characterized in the past as a "gigantic school" for citizenship,[6] proponents of the new technology promised significant social and political benefits. According to NBC founder David Sarnoff, television was "destined to provide greater knowledge to larger numbers of people, truer perception of the meaning of current events, more accurate appraisal of men in public life, and a broader understanding of the needs and aspirations of our fellow human beings."[7]

## The Early Years: Shared National Experiences

Television initially gave the wheel of nationalization and the power of mediation another spin in the same direction. In order to protect the viability of commercial television, the government limited competition and provided for the creation of only three national networks.

Television clearly operated in a broadcasting mode similar to that of previous media. The concept of "casting" was largely a one-way activity as broad-based networks cast out a message to a heterogeneous and largely inadvertent audience in the hope that a significant portion would find it appealing enough to tune in. The measures of success were subscription rates for newspapers, listeners for radio and ratings ("eyeballs" in the jargon of the insiders) for television.

Early television appealed to people who wanted to be informed and even more so entertained passively. "Part of the allure of television is the freedom from choice. It is a respite from an active world."[8] Television, like radio before it, is a one-way, one-to-many effort. It casts out content that is a "public good; that is costs do not increase when viewers are added...[and] larger audiences mean lower unit costs. Secondly, the message is valued by consumers in part because it is shared, and near simultaneity of receipt is an enhancement" provided by this sharing.[9]

In the early years, local affiliates ruled the roost, with national news programs not initiated until the late 1950s when NBC and CBS affiliates begrudgingly gave up 15 minutes of their valuable time for network news. ABC added evening network news programming a few years later. By 1963, all three networks expanded their evening news programs to one-half hour. Despite the limited national news window, an increasing percentage of the public began to look to television for its political news. A series of national accomplishments (such as landing men on the moon) and tragedies (such as the Kennedy assassination) led to shared islands of understanding. Even within the regular new programming, perceived interests of the audience and shared journalistic definitions of what was news led to considerable overlap in approach and content. On a typical evening one-third of the stories were carried by all three of the network news programs, one-third were carried by two of the three networks, and at most one-third of the stories were exclusives of one network.

From the 1960s to the 1980s, national political news was most effectively transmitted by the three television broadcast networks to a receptive audience. Of those attuned to television during prime time, over 80% were watching the networks during the 1980s. By the year 2000, that figure had dropped to below 50%.[10] Training in broadcast schools and the economic demands of creating and maintaining a large audience led to considerable overlap in what stories were chosen and how they were presented. Hot breaking stories were covered live with a large percentage of the population tuned in. In a similar vein, serious entertainment programs such as *Roots* became political education phenomena, with organizations having to cancel meetings since no one was willing to miss the next episode.

## Cabling for Competition

Frustration with the quality of broadcast signals in mountainous areas led to the creation of hard-wired cable systems intended to simply rebroadcast the limited range of commercial broadcast signals during the 1950s and 1960s. The technology created an excess of capacity for rebroadcasting existing signals. In the hope of expanding their market, cable companies began to look for value-added programming which they hoped would lure potential subscribers above and beyond those hampered by poor signal quality. The arrival of commercial satellite transmission of television signals in the mid-1970s offered an efficient method for the cable industry to transmit its own unique programming. Home Box Office hit the air in 1975, closely followed by Showtime, ESPN and Ted Turner's Channel 17. By the late 1970s the myriad of entertainment programs was joined by C-SPAN (Cable-Satellite Public Affairs Network), with the clear intention of providing the public with unvarnished access to political information.[11] CNN (Cable News Network) joined the mix in 1980, challenging the assumption that the public was not interested in a 24-hour news cycle.

The success of the cable's strategy was impressive. People would pay for television access, a commodity that had been introduced only a few decades earlier as a "free good," if they could not only get a better signal, but also get exclusive new programming. The number of cable companies grew from 1,335 to almost 8,000 by 1983.[12] The 20% of homes with access to cable in 1980 increased to over 50% in 1990 and over 70% by 1999.[13]

**Who Pays the Piper?** The drift toward cable television came largely at the expense of other media. For most of the potential audience, the time available for attentiveness to the media remains a "zero sum game" in which gains in one realm mean losses in another. The data are clear, print and scheduled network news audiences began to shrink. In 1985, almost 40% of households watched the network evening news programs. A decade later, that figure had dropped to 25%. Potential viewers were lured away by other programming or other pursuits. By 1998, 40% *of adults who watched* news programming depended primarily on one of the cable news channels and 57% relied on network broadcasts, but the trend lines favored cable news. The trend away from network news is even greater among younger individuals, the backbone of future audiences.[14]

In the battle for eyeballs, both commercial and cable networks began to fight back with their own new programming. The strict demarcations between information and entertained blurred to the degree that we had to coin a new term, "infotainment." Programs sought the title of "reality" television, and in the process blurred the line as to what was real and what was re-enacted. Network news programs took on a softer look with more human interest stories. CNN filled its screen with a gaggle of information boxes bombarding its viewers with a smorgasbord of facts and figures. Still the audiences moved away from hard news programming. While it is easy to point fingers at television executives, they point out they are only giving the public what it wants.

Despite moments of civic glory and eddies of excellence on the part of the television industry, as an audience we "are not knowledge seekers when we watch TV; we are couch potatoes." Rather than using television as a giant town meeting facilitating the education of all and the involvement of many, "it has become our Coliseum, where we all come together to watch others get torn apart."[15] *Survivor*, *The Mole* and *The Weakest Link*, are but the most recent examples of empty entertainment in which we vicariously and in a sanitized way "participate" more in the downfall of others, than the uplifting of the polity as a whole. While we might hope that television producers would appeal to our higher goals rather than pander to our lowest motives, there is little evidence we would rise to the bait and become hooked on more informative programming.

## The Consumer as an Individualized Producer

Cable television and the diversification of commercial television added one more component of choice, a much wider variety of programming options concerning *what* to watch. There developed an increasingly varied answer to the question "What's on TV tonight?" Two other technologies affected *what* one consumed by affecting *how* and *when* one watched. Traditional broadcast audiences were largely a passive entity "which received messages identically everywhere and helplessly responded." Contemporary audiences are now "active seekers, selectors and interpreters of media messages."[16]

**How We Watch.** The television "couch potatoes" so maligned during the 1980s lounged comfortably before the glowing screen as individuals explicitly eschewing physical exercise and denying themselves social contact. Walking around a neighborhood on a summer night, one looked through windows to see the glow of a television set and seldom saw people out on their porches and accessible for casual social interaction. Even if one was invited into an individual's social space, social norms did not require turning off the television to make room for conversation. At best, many visitors had to compete with the television as the primary focus of attention, inserting real two-way communication during commercials or gaps in the broadcast's one-way "munication." At worst, the visitors slinked away with the hollow promise that they would stop by at a more convenient time.

The introduction of the remote control individualized the television experience even more. The remote became the new "royal scepter" granting power and control. Trying to watch television with an inveterate channel surfer immediately clarifies who is in control and who is extra baggage. Even the term "channel surfer" exudes meaning. Surfing is an individual sport, with one person taking on the powerful waves. The only difference with the television remote lies in the fact that the waves are not physical but rather are successive sets of information signals with widely varying content. If the hand on the remote has a different pattern of patience and preference, the co-viewer experiences frustration. Disconnects over the remote break up many of the possibilities for some semblance of social interaction in watching television.

Generation and gender differences often drive the disconnect. Channel surfing is more common among younger viewers and men. Older viewers and females exhibit more loyalty to particular channels and programs. As comedian Jerry Seinfeld put it, "men hunt and women nest,"[17] although the power of generational differences has dramatically decreased the gender difference among younger viewers. Traditional viewers felt a responsibility to stick with "their" channel or program through boring segments and commercial breaks. They feared missing something, or felt they owed the advertisers attention since they paid for the program. Zapping out commercials and skipping segments is jarring. Younger viewers, brought up in the fast-paced era of multi-tasking, feel little discomfort surfing through dozens of channels before landing on one for a few minutes. If it engages them, they will stay, if not, it is off to catch the next programmatic wave. In many cases, surfers will intentionally "watch" two or three things at the same time, catching up on the baseball game score, seeing part of a music video on MTV, and getting the gist of a sitcom. Such peripatetic information retrieval can make sense to the person in charge of the remote, but seldom works for more than one person. The idea of the television (and earlier, the radio) being the focal point of the household, drawing families together for quality time and social interaction, is about as anachronistic as the old *Life* magazine photos of the whole family sitting around "watching" the radio and presumably acquiring common information to serve as the basis of quality conversation.

Seventy-six percent of American households today have two television sets, and 41% have three or more.[18] While some of this is the result of prosperity, the driving force is our unwillingness to use television as a collective good in which programming decisions are made by compromise and consensus. Families and housemates work out rules concerning control over the central television based on seniority, first on the scene, established schedule or might makes right. Those dissatisfied with the programming choice slither away, perhaps with a statement of disgust, to their own television, where they can be in control.

**When We Watch.** The VCR adds additional programming choices as we gain control over *when* we view television. By time-shifting our viewing to meet our convenience, we reduce the potential for creating a common information base for meaningful conversations with our fellow citizens. Asking colleagues "Did you see that program about crime last night?" is more than likely to be answered, "No, I taped it to watch this weekend," or "I watched a few minutes before moving on," than "Yes, and what they said about carjacking really bothered me." The first two answers do not portend the possibility of a meaningful conversation based on shared knowledge.

Emerging television-related technologies increase the potential for physical isolation and reduce shared knowledge. As more and more individuals walk around with hand-held wireless receivers, we become oblivious to those around us. "Rubbing shoulders" with our neighbors and colleagues takes on a whole new meaning as we try to avoid physical collisions as our primary focus remains on our souped-up hand-held video receiver. New technologies allowing viewers to stop and start broadcast signals at will decrease the potential of common viewing experiences and the consequent shared experiences and information. It is yet to be determined how the public will react. "Interactive television...may actually be less appealing to people...if they must invest more energy and imagination."[19]

## Television and Social Isolation

Critics of television's impact on social and political life go beyond concern over what and how we watch, honing in directly on the very act of watching itself. John L. Locke talks about people "isolat[ing] themselves in homes with television sets and other private amusements."[20] Robert Putnam describes televison as an "electronic technology [that] allows us to consume...hand-tailored entertainment in private, even utterly alone" and credits it as one of the prime reasons for the decline of "social capital," his term for the attitudes and behaviors that bind us together as a society.[21] As Mark Poster puts it, "Contemporary social relations seem to be devoid of a basic level of interactive practice which in the past was the matrix of democratizing politics; loci such as the agora, the New England town hall, the village church, the coffee house, the tavern, the public square, a convenient barn, a union hall, a park, a factory lunchroom, and even the street corner....The media, especially television but also other forms of electronic communication, isolate citizens from one another and substitute themselves for older spaces of politics."[22]

In emphasizing the personal dangers, it is asserted that time spent in front of the television is time unavailable for developing and strengthening social relationships. The preponderance of empirical analysis clearly indicates that television watching reduces social involvement.[23] Heavy television viewers tend to be more bored, lonely and unhappy. Since the bulk of research has only measured these factors at one point in time, it is not empirically verifiable whether unhappy and lonely people are drawn to television viewing, or whether the viewing itself has an independent impact on these attitudes.[24]

Even if television does not prove to be a cause of psychological maladies, the impact on the level of information one has available is significant. Even when controlling for important factors such as education, age and social ties, "those who *read* the news are more engaged and knowledgeable about the world than those who only *watch* the news."[25] Watching the news on television makes one more informed than not watching, but it is not more effective than more traditional media.

The impact of television viewing on political participation is also dramatic. As Putnam concludes, "dependence on television for entertainment is not merely *a* significant predictor of civic disengagement.

It is the *single most consistent* predictor that I have discovered."[26] Although it is possible that social and political isolates gravitate toward television viewing, the evidence seems to indicate more of a causal role as television "competes for scarce time," has "psychological effects that inhibit social participation," and includes "programmatic content...[that] undermines civic motivations."[27]

## Fragmentation: The First Shoe Drops

While nationalizing political experiences still occur, it is more difficult today to find events we as Americans have experienced similarly, particularly simultaneously through televison. With the expansion of television options, the movement away from television as an information source and the ability to become one's own scheduler by taping programs and time-shifting their ingestion, our common base of information has eroded. While we can still dredge up experiences like the slow-speed chase of O. J. Simpson's Bronco, scenes outside Columbine High School after the shooting, and the counting of contested ballots in Florida after the 2000 election, they are fewer, more diverse and usually less potent than those from previous years when a higher percentage of the population was paying attention to a more limited number of sources. With the exception of the terrorist attacks on the World Trade Center and the Pentagon, television has not created and probably will not create shared experiences for the new millennium anywhere to the degree that it did for the last half of the 20th century.

One measure of fragmentation is the percentage of the public following different news stories. Since 1986, the Pew Research Center for the People and the Press has identified the key news stories for each year and then asked national samples how closely they followed that story. While the inherent newsworthiness of stories obviously varies from year to year, between 1986 and 1990, the most closely watched stories were the 1986 Challenger disaster (80% of the population following it very closely), the 1989 San Francisco earthquake (73%), the 1992 verdict in the Rodney King case (70%), the 1996 crash of a Paris-bound TWA jet off New York (69%) and the 1987 rescue of a little girl in Texas from a well (69%). On the other end of the spectrum we find the 1999 Reform Party convention (1% of the public following it closely, the 1990 separation of Tom Cruise from his wife (2%), the 1992 Woody Allen marriage breakup or the Prince Charles–Lady Di marital problems (3%), and the 1998 story of whether former Chilean dictator August Pinochet should face trial (3%).[28] Given the broad range of years and stories it is instructive to consider the average level of attentiveness. Figure 4.2 summarizes the average percentage of adults following the top stories each year very closely. The pattern shows that the average story received less attention in later than in earlier years (see figure 4.2).

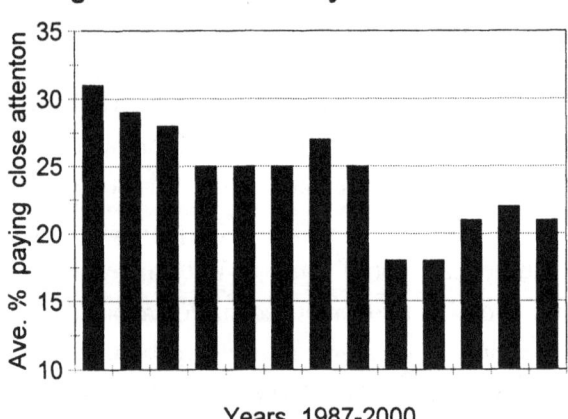

Figure 4.2. News Story Attentiveness

Years, 1987-2000

NOTE: Percentages indicate the percentage of adults paying close attention to the top stories of the year.

SOURCE: Surveys by the Pew Research Center for the People and the Press. Data available at *http://www.people-press.*

It is increasingly clear that television leads to both physical and substantive isolation. *Physical isolation* refers to the tendency of technologies to force people apart and reduce the potential for social interaction. Social interaction is a key component in promoting the form and content of political interaction. *Substantive isolation* refers to the declining commonality of shared facts, perceptions and political preferences. When the vast majority of citizens are exposed to the same basic core information, there is more room for coalition building and more potential for consensus and compromise. As citizens increasingly vary in the sources, content and interpretation of information, the potential for effective collective political action is challenged. The social and political consequences of either physical or social isolation is *fragmentation*, the direct opposite of community. In chapter 1 we discovered the decline of local geographic communities as individuals moved from living in communities of total commitment to living in communities of limited commitment.

It now seems clear that the first wave of new technologies, despite some initial but increasingly sporadic contributions to community building (contributions that supercede geography), also harbor within them community-challenging components.

# Chapter 5
# How Do You Know What You Know? Computers, the Internet and Beyond

> Technologies are not immutable, especially not computing ones. Their effects will be shaped by how they are constructed by engineers, how they are developed by service providers, and how they are used by consumers.
> —Robert Kraut et al., "Internet Paradox"

Technologies do not impact on individuals and social organizations like two ships without captains colliding at night. Once the course, speed and composition of the ships is determined, the results follow inexorable laws of physics whose variations from absolute predictability can only be determined by accounting for physical factors not originally taken into account. The impact of technologies on human organisms is more complex. Prediction involves an interaction between inherent tendencies of the technology (somewhat akin to the laws of physics) and the initial goals and behaviors of the affected human beings supplemented by the intentional and unintentional changes in course and reaction initiated by them.

New technologies have the potential to bring us together in virtual communities, facilitating the sharing of information, or to fragment our common information base expediting social isolation.[1] To a large degree, the impact is not one of either/or, but rather one of some of this and some of that. It is possible for conflicting consequences to coexist, with the subtle nature of one consequence affected by its seemingly opposite characterization.

## The Nature of the New Technologies as Information Providers

Technologies such as the Internet, Web, e-mail, databases and answering machines move users away from being *inadvertent audiences* who are broadcast *at*, to *intentional audiences* who *pick and choose* both the transmission medium and the content to which they pay attention. Radio and traditional television, without the remote and a vast array of options, involve a largely passive audience who often use the medium as little more than background noise. Print allows some choice of which articles to read, within the constraints of what editors and publishers decide to include. In a recent focus group on redesigning the *Baltimore Sun*'s local coverage pages, one very outspoken participant, who gloried in his lack of interest in local news, concluded, "The bottom line is that I don't really care what they do with the local section since I can take it or leave it. Now if you were talking about television news it would be a different story because there I am held hostage by what they decide to cover."

The Internet resembles a newspaper more than a broadcast medium, largely on the basis of choice. In actual operation, the Internet is used as a *narrow*casting medium with selective audiences seeking specialized content.

The new technologies inherently facilitate wider options and more narrowly crafted opportunities for users to *choose* the information they desire. One can decide which e-mails to open and even screen out those from particular sources. Surfing the Internet involves choosing which information "waves" to ride more than being buffeted around by what is sent in your direction by someone else.

As Bruce Owen describes it, "The Web surfer controls both the content and pace of arriving information....The television viewer gets to choose the channel and nothing else. Compared with television, the Internet gives people greater power to control information, reducing the danger of overload....The user not only chooses each screenful of images and words, but also decides how long that screen will stay active. To operate a Web browser, one must fiddle with mice and keyboards—participate in the experience. In most cases ones does not sit passively and let a Web page unfold."[2]

Web surfing is interactive and interactivity invites more involvement. Choosing to surf implies an interest in the information one discovers. Unsatisfactory information retrieval leads either to a new search strategy or going offline. There is no such thing as a passive, unresponsive surfer.

## Information Content

While it is deceptively incorrect to assume, as many do, that "everything worth knowing is available on the Internet" (or anyplace else for that matter), the lowered production and distribution costs combined with facilitated methods of searching increase the likelihood that a searcher will find the information he or she wants. With the constant expansion of sources, it is almost meaningless to indicate the number of Web sites or databases, since today's figures will be out of date by this evening.[3] Implying that we could once see clearly through the limited forest of freestanding trees of knowledge, David Shenk describes the current era as one of data "smog," where the glut of information overload is more pernicious than the lack of information.[4]

The language is even revealing. On databases or the Internet we "search" more than we "re-search" (search again). *Re*search implies searching a known path a second time. The concept of "reliability" in research results from two researchers following the same path and coming up with the same results. Knowledge is built by researchers replicating the work of others. Searching implies striking out on a new creative path based on the high expectation that something new of perceived use will be found. Searchers seldom follow the same path as others or repeat paths taken in the past. Searching is most appropriate in relatively unexplored realms and/or when creativity seems more fruitful than validation. The technology tends to lead searchers to view all exploration as a creative endeavor.

Web information seekers exemplify Marshall McLuhan's "nomadic gatherers of knowledge."[5] Rather than following a hierarchical searching pattern, the nomads come upon information more idiosyncratically and then follow multiple links to narrow in on what they really want. In the process they are often diverted into information realms they had not considered and these become sources themselves as they forward material to others or capture it to their own Web site. The "open architecture" philosophy of many Internet activists asserts the right to use, transform and distribute whatever they find on the Web. The fact that congressional information has already been paid for by the public and is not copyrighted gives further impetus to this presumed right. This "snatch and grab" or "right click acquisition" approach scares those wishing to control information. Not only do information seekers not enter the information realms in clearly predictable ways, but once there they often have the power to download what they find, edit it and send it on its way without the cost of traditional publication technologies. The newly transformed information may well look official, but it is out of the control of the originator.

The danger of information overload and the focus on the unique or arcane is real. To some degree computers are more like pumps than filters. They accelerate the transmission of large amounts of data, with only minimum ability to help us better select and organize the data into useful information and eventual knowledge. Searching leads more to the discovery of *data* than to *information*. Data are the bits of truth that creative analysts combine into *in-formation* (bits of data in a useful pattern). The numbers 28, 21, 36 and 20 as well as the terms "Cowboys," "Ravens, "Vikings" and "Eagles" are bits of data. They turn into information when we link them to reveal that the Cowboys beat the Vikings, 18 to 21, and the Ravens beat the Eagles, 36 to 20.

"Education, which comes from the Latin *educare*, meaning to raise and nurture, is more a matter of imparting values and critical thinking than inputting raw data. Education is about enlightenment, not just access....Education can not be fixed with a digital pipeline of data."[6] The trick for us as individuals and as a society is to increase our capabilities for creating and evaluating information. Technology becomes one tool we might harness in that task.

## Information Quality

Technology does not guarantee veracity of information. Millions of pieces of misinformation and misperceptions have appeared in print and have been broadcast over radio and television. The relatively low cost of publishing on the Web, the reduced role of the editorial function (a quality-control device largely dictated by the cost of production) and the broad instantaneous ability to search and retrieve on the Internet increases the likelihood that misinformation will reach its target in a timely fashion.

**Judging by the Source.** The danger of misinformation is exacerbated by aspects of new technologies which allow the true sources of information to hide their identity. For example, the Internet address system facilitates anonymity. On the aggregate level, e-mail addresses don't allow demographic grouping such as that facilitated by zip codes. The extensions on e-mail addresses (.edu, .gov, .com, etc.) give only vague clues as to the source.

On the individual level, aliases allow one to both hide one's identity and/or signal one's preferred, if unrealistic, persona. One of my students with political ambitions signs on as "thePrezisme," a clear statement of ambition. Anonymity is a dual-edged sword. On the one hand it is freeing; it allows one's messages to be reacted to for their content alone if one's Internet "handle" ( to use terminology of citizens band radio) is ambiguous enough. The cues given by one's gender, race or clothing in a face-to-face conversation are erased. For the sender, intentional misrepresentation potentially provides a new experience and possibly new insights Males can find out what it feels like to communicate as a female. Old people can see how others react to them when thinking they are young. For many, the Internet becomes a giant sandbox of fraudulent role playing.

While much of the role playing can be seen as innocent fun, at least in the political realm, rights must be linked with responsibilities. The possibility of anonymity "is exciting because a worldly connection can be made with unknown others...[and] no responsibility has to be taken for its consequences."[7] Anonymous e-mail and the use of aliases undermines the ability to assign responsibility and may well encourage irresponsibility. Similarly, it is often difficult to determine who is responsible for the content on a particular Web site and thereby get a clue to its probable veracity. True sponsors often hide behind appealing but meaningless names.

Standing up and being counted in politics assumes enough commitment to one's cause to take responsibility for one's action. Anonymous shots across the public's bow have less legitimacy than heartfelt preferences communicated in such a way that a political give-and-take can occur among honest and forthright participants. In the deliberative democracy model, ideas are put forward, debated and refined. Such interaction is severely hampered by participants unwilling to put their identity where their mouth is.

**Bias.** Despite its relatively lower production costs, not all ideas or viewpoints find their way onto the Internet in proportion to their validity, creativity, distribution in the population, or any other objective measure of their worth. Like other media, the Internet suffers from both *intentional bias* and *structural bias*. Intentional bias occurs when information disseminators post messages designed to promote a particular point of view. Many Web sites, chat rooms, and bulletin boards are intentionally postings "with an attitude." They exist to persuade, not to present an objective view of the world. Structural bias occurs when a medium draws certain kinds of users because of unequal familiarity, skills or resources. Even though Web sites are relatively inexpensive to create, there are still skill and resource thresholds which block some potential users. Even after breaking in, those groups and individuals with more resources have an advantage in creating more appealing sites by harnessing the newest "bells and whistles," and by designing them in such ways as to be more likely to be picked up by search engines.

In some Internet realms, the bias is palpable and complex. Using a combination of survey data and content analysis, Hill and Hughes point out an interesting contradiction. Demographically, "Internet *activists* (those who use the Internet regularly) as a group are actually more Democratic and liberal than the public at large." On the other hand, "the actual *content* of the Usenet newsgroups, chat rooms and the World Wide Web's political areas [are] in fact dominated by conservative ideas....Politics on the Internet is dominated by a relatively small, though vociferous and technologically savvy, conservative minority."[8] Thus the demographics would suggest one likely bias, yet the skills and activity level of a small portion of the conservative posters lead to substantive bias in another direction. The technology itself does not preordain a particular kind of bias, nor does it innoculate information recipients from receiving biased information.

**Putting the "Co" into Communication.** As discussed in chapter 3, much of what passes for communication is really one-way "municating." Traditional broadcast technologies usually lack the interactivity of a true conversation. While the old-time radio announcers might plead for listeners to "keep those cards and letters coming in," broadcast television and print media can only assume that viewers and readers are receiving the messages they broadcast.

Face-to-face communications are enhanced through facial expressions and body language. It is almost always clear whether the message is getting through. Follow-up questions providing more depth of meaning are easier to pose and more difficult to duck. "Oral discourse, especially the face-to-face variety, is less inhibited. The speaker's intentions may still be message-oriented, but things come out that he had not planned to disclose."[9]

E-mail and chat rooms fall somewhere between formal written communications and oral discourse in terms of the strategic sensitivity of the participants and the potential for interactivity. "Instant messaging" adds immediacy and increases the potential potency of the message. It is yet unclear whether on-line technologies will enhance political communications. After an extensive empirical study focusing on the users and content of on-line discussions, Richard Davis concludes that political communication on the Internet is far from reaching its potential.[10] On-line political discussion tends to be pursued by unrepresentative and unaccountable participants whose extreme views are not organized or tempered by a moderator. Rather than engaging in a political conversation designed to reach a thoughtful, deliberative conclusion, participants tend to blurt out their views and blot out any response that disagrees with their views. There is little attempt to come to any consensus through bargaining and/or refinement of perspectives. At best, participants agree to disagree. At worst, the dominant point of view simply drives those in disagreement away. With no necessity of an awkward physical departure, those whose views are rejected often simply slink away with an anonymous click of their mouse.

**Triumph of Form over Content.** The problem of potential misinformation is exacerbated by the fact that format may imply legitimacy to the less informed. If seeing is believing, seeing information on a Web page with fancy graphics may lead to the conclusion that if they have gone to so much trouble presenting the ideas this professionally, they must be true. Just as in the early days of computers when those in awe of the technology almost stood up and saluted printouts, it is difficult for many to peer beyond information presentation to take a peek at validity. Format alone can take "sow's ear" data and turn it into seemingly "silk purse" information.

**Breaking the "Containers" of Knowledge.** Political entities such as nation-states were once legitimately viewed as "containers," defining and limiting legitimate and useful political interactions. For most citizens, life as they knew it stopped at the legally defined geographic borders. Broadcast media of either the electronic or print variety seldom had any intention of audiences beyond national borders. Most other social and economic entities constrained themselves to established geographic borders largely because of legal constraints.

The emergence of new social entities such as multinational corporations and non-governmental organizations (NGOs) both encouraged and were encouraged by new technologies. Geographic borders became increasingly irrelevant and the power of information showed its true potency. The Berlin Wall, a classic symbol of an attempt to limit human interaction with a physical boundary, was not torn down by tanks or bombs, but succumbed to the power of ideas transmitted by satellite dishes.

Computer networks do not honor physical boundaries. They can only be forced, with intimidation of users and/or the difficult introduction of sophisticated screening devices, to block certain kinds of messages or messages from specified sources. Where a message originated is almost transparent to the e-mail or Internet user. Countries such as China and Singapore, wishing to shield their populations through the deployment of electronic "Berlin Walls," face public degradation for their seemingly unrealistic attempt to swim against the tide of history and technology.

While it is true that the Internet ignores national boundaries, with cyberspace existing as "a realm without borders," the days of the nation-state are not necessarily numbered. "The Internet undoubtedly creates new difficulties for nation-states asserting their sovereign authority, but the aspects of the Internet that now evade national jurisdictions are unlikely to be the foundations for a worldwide erosion of power of the nation-state." While the Internet does make it more difficult to shield a country's citizens from cross-border information flows and it "will be more difficult to run a closed society and still benefit from the fruits of modern technology....Nation-states have been around for a long time, and they possess deep reservoirs of power and legitimacy."[11]

With new technology, nation-states are better viewed as "transmission-belt" organizations than as "containers." Their primary use lies in underwriting and facilitating the flow of information, much of which will rightfully be used by recipients outside the geographic boundaries in which it was created. Geographically defined political entities are forced to define the role they want to play in the increasingly borderless world, both in terms of what information they wish to export and which information will be imported to become part of their important, but reduced realm of state-based decision-making.[12]

**Cyber-tracking.** The technology itself provides at least one tool for countering misinformation. Politics has historically been an oral tradition in America, from public orations to cracker barrel conversations. Even for the most famous of our oral traditions, such as the Lincoln-Douglas debates, there remains some controversy over whose transcription actually captured what was said. Most political conversations were not recorded. Even when records were kept, only a minuscule proportion of historical documents and published newspapers remain. In the past and today, both politicians and their supporters often leave meetings with different versions of what was said and what was agreed to. Even the public record may be misleading. The decision-making process in the contemporary Congress is greased by the realization that members can reconsider what they said on the floor before it is entered into the permanent record. Members end their comments with the request to "revise and extend" their remarks.

Faulty memories, differing interpretations and the ability to make subtle changes in one's position make it easier to come to a face-saving compromise with an antagonist. New technologies provide full and faithful recording and searching of political discourse. Putting cameras in the chambers of Congress made it more embarrassing for members to change their positions. Digitizing records reduces archival costs, encouraging the retention of records that would have dropped into the ash bins of history in the past. Technologies allowing full-text searching mean that today less can be done by stealth.

Written communications have more readily been accepted as evidence of what a person really wants to say "for the record." Lawyers and individuals alike strategize over what they are willing to commit to paper and how they are willing to present it. In the early days of e-mail, it was treated more like oral conversation than written communication. The anonymity of facing a CRT screen freed some inhibitions and led to "flaming" (personal attack) comments which one would not make in a face-to-face conversation and which one was unlikely to commit to writing. Flaming may well have decreased as individuals became accustomed to the new medium. In 1995, almost 70% of adults with access to computers indicated that e-mail led to "more frank" communications. By 1998, only 38% characterized e-mail in that way, with 55% saying it "makes no difference" in terms of frankness.[13] E-mail "shots from the hip" were seen as transitory and ephemeral—until they began to come back and wound the sender.

While the legal status of e-mail access by law enforcement officials and the ownership rights of e-mail messages are still being defined by the courts, wise users recognize that they should not say anything on e-mail they would not want public. Publicizing a damaging e-mail message or including a document on the Web may well be enough to do harm. When a former boyfriend of conservative talk-show host "Dr. Laura" (Schlesinger) published nude photos of her on a Web site, the courts found themselves unable to control the distribution and undo the harm. The concrete nature of an e-mail message once printed endows it with the legitimacy of a written document. Even more than an oral message that can't be taken back once spoken, the "unringing" of an e-mail or Web site "bell" is even more difficult.

Increasing sophistication of users has tempered usage patterns and moved e-mail more toward the written communication end of the scale as users realize that e-mail has the permanence of written documents. Even the "delete" key may not erase an e-mail message forever. As Oliver North found out the hard way, the permanence of shredded documents pales in comparison to electronic backup files.[14] The courts of law and of public opinion accept e-mail as a true and valid record of communications. The shift from face-to-face or telephone communications to e-mail and other computer-mediated communication technologies creates a permanent record which can allow one to check what was actually said or written.

The lack of a clear record allows for self-serving revision. Having one's words thrown back into one's face hardens positions. The positive side of the increased tendency to retain records and the ability to search them is a reduction of duplicity and the increased expectation that one must be accountable for one's words. On the other hand, such precision recall can lock a person into an untenable position, denying him or her a face-saving retreat. With technology "ideas can become concretized before they are fully developed through the give and take of freewheeling dialogue."[15]

On the personal level, the new technologies challenge one's privacy. Society has long been awash with data about individuals. We leave multiple "tracks" as we shop, make telephone calls, check books out of the library and do a myriad of everyday activities. For most of human history such tracks were easily covered by disuse or inaccessibility. In other words, the discrete bits of data were impossible to reassemble into useful information (disparate data placed in order as "in-formation"). Modern computer technology has "made it possible to combine these bits...in new ways, rapidly and inexpensively. A simple database and search program, for example, can match demographics, economic, and geographical information to give remarkably precise accounts about consumption patterns....There is an intimate link between information and identity; the information that others have about us also defines who we are."[16]

**The Bottom Line on Content.** A better-informed citizenry is more likely when there is more information rather than less. The challenge of the cyber-information age lies not in limiting information but rather in equipping the end users with the tools for finding the most useful information and evaluating its veracity.

**Information Discovery**

The existence of relevant information means little unless there is the marriage of a receptive seeker and a piece of information perceived as useful. There are many opportunities for missed connections. The information seeker may not have access to or find the source.

**Search and Deploy.** Despite dramatic growth in access, a large and demographically unrepresentative segment of society remains blocked on the entrance ramp of the information superhighway. Although 45% of individuals in 1999 claimed they had access to the Internet at home,[17] this figure over-represents the wealthier and better-educated segments of society.

Beyond the large differences in access to computers in general and the Internet in particular, access to search engines and their utility vary widely. The inclusion and exclusion rules of the most widely used of the free search engines bring considerably different results. A search (admittedly egocentric). under my rather unique surname found 672 hits in Lycos, 450 in Alta Vista, 410 in Yahoo and 140 in GoTo. Each engine has different rules for what is searched and how it is presented. Some search engines emphasize searching titles and abstracts, while others give equal weight to the full content. The inclusion and exclusion rules are seldom clearly outlined to the potential user. A number of search engines accept payments for better placement in searches. Lists of "top ten hits" over-represent those who pay for placement or who have bought advertising on the site.

The ability to search commercial databases varies even more along demographic lines. I "read" over 4,000 newspapers and journals every day because my home educational institution subscribes to LEXIS-NEXIS. I allow the computer to do a pre-determined search for new articles about a subscribed set of topics. Despite my addiction to the information, it is not a service I could afford if it were not subsidized by my employers. The "digital divide," which separates those with access to computerized information from those without, begins at the point where individuals have a chance to discover the very *existence* of information, well before they must make a decision about their need to access it.

**Access.** Until the age of full-text searching of computer databases, *physical access* (actually getting a copy) to a book or article was the necessary initial step to *content access* (finding out what was in the book or document). Using hard-copy documents involves either physical scanning (reading word for word or skimming) or relying on content access tools provided by others (tables of contents, indexes, etc.). In the mid-1960s, Jonathon Robbin "first conceived that computers could be used for more than lightning-quick calculations....[T]hey could be programmed to juxtapose enormous amounts of otherwise unwieldy data in order to achieve a new degree of pattern recognition."[18] No longer was the searcher limited by the skill, creativity and intellectual map of the author or indexer. Physical access was no longer necessary as long as there was electronic access and a good search engine. Searches could be done on the basis of multiple criteria, paring down a mountain of raw material into successively smaller piles each with a higher percentage of informational "wheat" and a declining percentage of irrelevant "chaff." It developed a whole new way of thinking. I never realized the intellectual shift until I began using a traditional index to find a quote which mentioned a series of presidential advisers. I fired up my manual computer (my brain and senses) looking up the page references for each of the known names. I then looked for overlap in page numbers to create a Boolean approach (this name *and* that name mentioned on the same page). Lacking complete overlap of the three names, I feared I would not find the quote, only to discover the frailty of the indexer, who had missed one name for indexing on the crucial page. A good search engine used on an electronic document would not have made such a mistake.

**Distractions.** Information technologies are more than tools for helping us navigate through large bodies of data. They are often created with individual and societal needs in mind and in turn come to reflect, reinforce and re-energize needs and perspectives. In Heidegger's terminology, technologies "enframe" a culture, revealing and exemplifying its basic values and outlooks.[19]

For example, the Windows computer environment exemplifies the multi-tasking nature of modern society. In Windows, one can have a number of sites and/or documents open at the same time. It is like having a desk filled with paper documents and shifting from one to the other at will. Rather than emphasizing the alternative view of doing *one* thing and doing it well, the Windows outlook and functionality legitimize paying partial attention to multiple tasks.

As I write these words, my e-mail is up and going so I can check it after each paragraph (unless I get curious more often). In another corner of the screen a video feed, silent for the moment, monitors C-SPAN or CNN, assuring that I don't miss anything they deem important. Unless disabled, some e-mail systems provide an audio alert when e-mail is waiting. Few fail to succumb to the temptation and ignore it. As Nelson Thall, research director at the University of Toronto's Marshall McLuhan Center, puts it, "Man wakes up today and electronic technology speeds up his mind....Your mind is empowered with the ability to float out into the electronic void, being everywhere at once....Physical borders that for tens of thousands of years have helped define who we are, are fast becoming obsolete. We can 'go' almost anywhere at any time, in the virtual world."[20]

Rather than taking the approach of "once a task has begun, do not leave it till it's done," it entices one to pick away at tasks in a serial manner, arguing that efficiency comes from "striking while the iron is hot," not digging in and finishing a task in some pre-determined, prioritized order. There is a great temptation for the flashy and fun tasks to overwhelm the necessary but mundane tasks. At the moment, I am trying to finish this paragraph rather than going back to one more game of Free Cell or seeing if anyone is on my instant messaging.

Word processing is another technology which frees one to circumvent the traditional linear manner of production. There is no penalty for shopping around a document to add, delete or correct. Creating a document on a typewriter was a linear process in which all of one's thoughts had to be worked out ahead of time to avoid multiple drafts. Insertions or deletions required scrapping the entire document and beginning again. As I write this paragraph I have little idea where it will be placed in the final text. All I know is that, if it proves to be well argued, it will fit in somewhere and that I am not being inefficient by writing it while the ideas are on my mind. I can simply block and move it where it best fits without any need to rekey the words. Five minutes ago I was working on another very different document, and I am unconsciously (Oh! Oh! Now it has become conscious) thinking about where I will go with it next. I can hardly wait to finish this paragraph so I can click back to the previous one with my newly surfaced insight.

**Catching Our Attention.** The glut of information requires information purveyors to increasingly work harder to get our attention. E-mails come with provocative subject lines ("sex," "free money," "secret" and "read this") to make sure they are opened. The sender continues without embarrassment justifying the deceit by saying, "Now that I have your attention." Political information competes with a multitude of often more appealing stimuli. "The increasingly mean-spirited election campaigns merely reflect a society where hyperbole, vulgarity, and ostentation thrive" in order to cut through the more mundane and thoughtful information missiles.[21] If they could be assured of the impact of their message on voters, few candidates would prefer the visually outrageous and substantively bereft messages of the modern campaign.

As in many realms, "he who pays the piper calls the tune." Although the debate of the 1980s as to whether we should "allow" commercialization of the Internet seems rather quaint today, it is important to remember what we have lost in the mad rush to finance Web-site development and "free" e-mail service on the back of commercial interests. "The growing commercialization of the Internet means that edifying local and educational materials are buried under advertising banners."[22]

The ability of senders to secure our attention through enticing words, impressive graphics or audio attention-getters increases the likelihood we will attune to *their* message rather than to that of someone else. Some Web sites "grab" their users and deactivate the "back" button, giving new meaning to the Web as an entangling phenomenon inhibiting our movement at will.

Once a Web site has drawn our intentional or unintentional attention, we leave a record of our visit (a so-called "cookie"), indicating which sites we visited and for how long. With our machine and/or e-mail address captured, the Web-site owner can then send us unsolicited messages whenever we are on line, making us the target of a broadcast format and turning us back into an unintentional audience for information we may well not want.

## The Time Trap

New technologies fail to respect space or time. Distance once slowed down the arrival of information via the mail. The routines of the mail arriving at a particular time and the norms of not placing telephone calls before 8 a.m. or after 10 p.m. help structure one's activities and provide for mandatory isolation—and perhaps even serious contemplation. E-mail allows, and for some even demands, individuals to be on call 24/7/365 (24 hours a day, 7 days a week, 365 days a year). Senders of e-mail have the option of monitoring whether their message has been opened yet. Tardy treatment of one's e-mail, now often measured in hours rather than days, may well result in a follow-up message. Regular e-mail users have crafted well thought out follow-up messages ("I have been having trouble with my e-mail and just thought I would check to see if you got my last message") so they will not sound too insistent.

The Web and cable television news both facilitate timeliness and are promoted for their ability to capture and transmit breaking news. Survey data indicate a greater interest by the public in breaking news.[23] The extreme case of timeliness is the presence of Web cameras waiting for something to happen. Technology has finally caught up with McLuhan's insightful observation that "instant information creates involvement."[24]

Technology affects one's time horizons. Much more of life is carried on in real time. While this development reduces frustrating waits for information and the consequences of our decisions, the results are not all positive. The ability to acquire and transmit information instantaneously tends to "overload people with information about current developments, narrow their focus, and pressure them to act quickly....People seem captivated by an intense awareness of the immediate present and its crises, a sense of detachment from the past, and an anticipation of an accelerating rush into the future...[and] information (not to mention disinformation) is flowing faster than many people feel they can absorb, sort, make decisions, and obtain additional information that may be needed to make the right decision and control the outcome."[25]

For example, ordering airline tickets on line forces instantaneous decisions without full information for fear of losing a great fare through delay. While one might want to mull over the schedule or check out the options with one's traveling companions, the cut-rate ticket options almost scream, "Grab this fare now or you will probably lose it the next time you log on."

## Privatizing and Fragmenting Tendencies

Withdrawal from the human community is not a new phenomenon. As we saw in chapter 2, geographic mobility cuts our anchor lines with a clearly identifiable set of neighbors. Each new wave of technology has provided more options for isolation. The early era of families viewing television as a social group has largely been replaced by the individual couch potato, grasping his or her remote and controlling the television set in a household. Controlling the remote is tantamount to having a royal scepter granting ownership of the television. In one-television households, children are often scheduled for their day to be in control. In the era of multiple sets, those unhappy with the choice of the person with the remote often strike out to another television set where they can be king or queen of choice. Physical isolation not only undermines social interaction, but also the limits the potential for developing a shared base of information.

**PC (Personal Computer) = PI (Personal Isolation).** The computer is even more of a one-on-one machine. It is almost impossible to look over the shoulder of the primary user and become comfortably and fully engaged. "The global village predicted by the seers in the 1960s is being replaced by electronic cottages populated by isolated dreamers. We do not know our neighbors....We are a nation of lonely molecules."[26]

Empirical data on actual utilization indicates that Internet activity and social interaction are clearly a zero-sum game. Norman Nie, chief investigator of a major study on the societal impact of the Internet, concludes that "the more hours people use the Internet, the less time they spend with real human beings." Countering the arguments that the Internet will compensate by creating more meaningful virtual communities, Nie and his co-author, Lutz Erbring, argue that there was "no evidence that virtual communities would provide a substitute for traditional human relationships....When you spend your time on the Internet, you don't hear a human voice and you never get a hug."[27] They found that Internet users spend much less time on the telephone to friends and family, concluding that "Internet time is coming out of time viewing television but also at the expense of time people spend on the phone gabbing with family and friends or having a conversation with people in the room with them." In a more dire tone, they assert, "The Internet could be the ultimate isolating technology that further reduces our participation in communities even more than television did before it. [The Internet] is not like TV, which you can treat as background noise. It requires more engagement and attention."[28]

The public does not seem to be too concerned about the fragmentation tendencies. When asked if the computer was a "good thing because it brings together people with similar interests," or a "bad thing because it brings together people who share dangerous ideas," 54% said a "good thing" compared to 28% describing it as a "bad thing."[29]

Using over-time data on new Internet users, Kraut et al. found that "greater use of the Internet was associated with declines in the participant's communication with family members in the household, declines in the size of their social circle and increases in their depression and loneliness."[30]

Their findings clearly indicate Internet use as the cause of these changes since their methodology held constant initial demographic, communications, social interaction, and psychological variables which could have been seen as independent causes themselves. "Ironically, just as cyberspace can bring a world of strangers to one's computer screen, so can it lead one to withdraw from physical society."[31]

As J. McClellan concludes, "Rather than providing a replacement for the crumbling public realm, virtual communities are actually contributing to its decline. They're another thing keeping people indoors and off the streets. Just as TV produces couch potatoes, so on-line culture creates mouse potatoes, people who hide from real life and spend their whole life goofing off in cyberspace."[32]

**Other Privatizing Technologies.** It is not just the computer as a delivery device that has the potential for privatizing our information sources. Other technologies, some facilitated by computers, contribute also.

Answering machines have become tools for avoiding social interaction. Although initially created to facilitate interaction by making sure we do not miss a call, answering machines are increasingly being used to do what would be socially suicidal in face-to-face communication or in real-time answering of the phone, deciding whether or not to respond to the voice of our closest friends. Ignoring someone hailing us on the street, or picking up the phone and after a few seconds saying. "Oh, it's you. I don't want to talk," sends a signal that makes future communication quite unlikely. Screening our calls allows us to choose with whom to talk without threatening future conversations.

Looking at the answering machine from the other end of the line, it also has privatizing potential for the sender of messages. If we want to avoid telling people embarrassing or unpleasant things in person, we can always call their answering machine at a time we assume they are not at home.[33] We drop the information "bomb" and then slither off without confrontation.

"Caller ID" allows one to screen information inputs in real time. One can either pick up the phone and allow the caller to win this round of "telephone tag" or leave the unwanted caller hanging there, not knowing if the intended recipient is available. One never knows when a user of caller ID has rejected a conversation because of who is calling. On the other hand, the person who favors us by picking up the phone and calling us by name after identifying us as the caller boosts our ego by sending the message, "I don't want to talk to all the rest of those pests, but you are special."

New phones allow the user to pre-set the ringing tone based on the source of the incoming call. Instantaneously, one can choose whether they want to pick it up or let it switch over to voice mail, where it sits in limbo at the wish and whim of the intended recipient.

"Call waiting" sends a different kind of privatizing message. While we have all been in face-to-face conversations where the person with whom we are talking seems to be scanning the room for a better prospect and eventually extricates himself or herself to move on, it is usually done with some grace. Call waiting also provides the opportunity to "trade up" our conversation partners. It both creates a less equal opportunity structure and operates in a context where its users have yet to develop well-entrenched norms and strategies for gracefully breaking off a conversation. The conversation participant getting a second call is in the driver's seat since he or she is the one important enough to be interrupted. One has a chance to check out the source while leaving the other participant hanging onto a dead line, twiddling thumbs, with nothing to do. When the person receiving the second call comes back, he or she has the option of verifying the initial participant's value by saying,"Oh, that was nothing important. What was it you were saying?" or even more of a stroke to one's ego, "That was the While House calling about my invitation to stay in the Lincoln bedroom, but I told them they would have to get back to me after I found out how you managed to solve your hangnail problem." On the other hand, call waiting can signal minor ("Sorry, I have to run; one of my kids is having car trouble") or major ("Goodbye, I can't wait to talk to this vinyl-siding telemarketer who calls every night at dinner time") disinterest in continuing the initial conversation. The basis for a good conversation is having the undivided attention of your target audience. Call waiting clearly sends the signal that one is willing to talk to that caller until a better option comes along. Some people have a self-defense strategy of using a little white lie to alert a conversation partner: "I am expecting an important call, but let's talk until it comes in." This strategy allows the users to break off the conversation at any time they lose interest by saying, "Oops, here comes that call; nice to talk to you. Click." Being dropped from a conversation by a user of call waiting chills one's interest in future conversations with that individual.

For the outside caller, call waiting can also send a number of signals. A busy signal from someone without call waiting sends a neutral message at worse: "So and so is pretty busy, I hope I can get through at another time." Some callers may view the situation as more of a judgment on themselves: "So and so must be pretty important since they get so many calls. I will be lucky to get through next time." With call waiting, the new caller is at the mercy of the intended recipient; after being told, "I am on the other line," he or she is momentarily held in limbo, silently pleading, "Pick me; pick me," while the recipient decides whether to come back to the new caller or not. Even when new callers are told, "I will be right back to you," they are not immune to discomfort since they don't know what is being said to the person on the other line. There is the temptation to assume that the previous conversation is being cut off by saying to the original caller, "I have this pest on the other line; I can't get off easily. I will call you back as soon as I am free."

These telephone technologies serve as the bricks in our "protections against useless information" fortress, selectively allowing some sources and their attendant information through while keeping us in splendid isolation concerning messages from others. A well-designed wall would serve us well, but there is always the danger that we will miss out on what is on the other side to our detriment.

## Information Isolation

Social insolation brings with it a host of potential problems, the bulk of which are well beyond our discussion. Our concern is with one narrow, albeit very politically important component, information isolation.

Traditional print and electronic media is based on a broadcast mode, where a source delivers a package of information which a consumer must sort through using limited and imperfect devices to determine what to absorb and what to ignore. Newspaper readers prioritize and scan different sections of the paper and choose those to read based on titles and past experiences as to which sections are likely to include stories in which they are interested. Headlines and lead paragraphs signal the content. Some newspapers use simple indexes to guide the reader and utilize story placement and headline size to signal to the reader what *they* think is important. The user of traditional electronic media chooses networks and programs in order to receive certain kinds of stories. Once a set of stories begins to flow through a newscast, the only choice for the viewer is to pay attention, tune out a story, or change the channel. The imperfect nature of screening and choice leads to a significant potential that the end users will receive information they did not intend to absorb.

Internet and database searching is quite different. We assume up front that we know what we need to know and show great faith in both our own ability to predict our needs and the capability of information indexers to match our predetermined categories with new information that comes along. "When someone looks for information on the Nets, they are seeking answers to specific questions or information about specific topics."[34] To be sure, some "leakage" occurs as we are lured way by advertising banners and/or headline teasers only to inadvertently pick up information outside our normal channels. In general, it is increasingly possible to exist in a self-defined and self-confining bubble-like echo chamber, receiving information on a very limited number of topics, and to potentially limit that information to one particular ideological take on the issue. To the degree the Net or database user knows where to look and knows the questions to ask, the information search is considerably more efficient. But efficiency is not an end all and be all. What they miss is serendipitously coming across information beyond their self-imposed radar screen and information so cleverly packaged that it becomes a shared information resource on which conversations with others can be built. Serendipity is destiny for the individuals seeking to broaden their information base. The new technologies, on the other hand, have been largely utilized to narrow rather than broaden one's search. Such capacity gives new and dangerous meaning to the old quip, "My mind is made up; don't confuse me with the facts." In the new information age, the quip becomes even more restrictive; "My mind is made up. I don't even realize there are potentially conflicting facts."

A Usenet group on the Internet "is not only a means of communicating, it is a place where people can connect with others, share their views, and, potentially, develop their political beliefs." In reality, Usenet participants are self-selected. But as far as exposing participants to new ideas, Usenet participation "is something people use to reinforce beliefs they have already developed....[they] serve to protect their [participants,] dominant point of view from those who may disagree."[35] The electronic echo chamber has the potential for reinforcing true believers more than fostering critical thinkers.

Even the process of saving a discovered site as a "bookmark" or a "favorite" contributes to the self-imposed information blinders we place on ourselves. Almost 60% of Internet users maintain bookmarks.[36] Bookmarks efficiently lead us back to sites containing information we have found useful in the past, but they often do not facilitate broadening our information base. Even when sites invite us to go out and explore by providing links to other sites, it is the rare site that encourages links providing exposure to contradictory information. Using an empirical analysis of 60 political Web sites, Cass Susstein found that only 15% provided links to sites with opposing views whereas almost 60% limited their links to like-minded sites.[37] This confirms the conclusion that "far from fostering deliberative political discourse, most of the surveyed Web sites sought to consolidate speech power and served to balkanize the public forum."[38]

We increasing live in a "niche culture" where we seek out and acquire more and more narrow personal databases of information.[39] Our knowledge-gathering and utilization patterns closely resemble that of a post hole digger (digging deeper and deeper knowledge about an increasingly narrow set of topics) as opposed to a fence stringer (remaining at the surface, but tying together disparate manifestations of deeper meaning into a useful pattern). The technology has the potential for undermining the information we need for a meaningful shared discourse necessary to maintain democracy in a pluralistic culture.[40]

## The Potential for Virtual Communities

Not all projections are dire eulogies for democracy hastened to its death by privatizing technologies. According to some writers, virtual communities facilitated by new technology are "exciting new forms of community which *liberate* the individual from the social constraints of embodied identity and from the restrictions of geographically embodied space; which *equalize* through the removal of embodied hierarchical structures; and which promote a sense of connectedness (or *fraternity*) among interactive participants."[41] In the early stages of the Internet, Howard Rheingold saw technology as having an additive impact, expanding human contact; he argued that "People's social networks do not consist only of people they see face to face. In fact social networks have been expanding because of artificial media since the printing press and the telephone."[42] Almost a quarter of Americans using the Internet claim to have made a friend on line.[43] Sociologist Amitai Etzioni argues that while people using more technology have less time to spend with other people, they do "form very strong relations over the Internet, and many of them are relations that they could not find in any other way."[44]

While there are clear examples of vibrant and politically effective virtual communities developing using e-mail and Web pages,[45] portraying them as the desirable or probable model for the future of democracy rather than unique exceptions has led a number of observers to raise serious objections.[46]

**Anonymity and Misleading Identity.** In face-to-face communities individuals present themselves to others by necessity as they actually are. Race, gender, physical appearance, accent, etc. help form first impressions which may carry a great deal of substantive baggage from both sides of the communications relationship. In physical communities we label people based on their ascriptive characteristics (African American, Arab American, soccer mom, etc.). The new participants may feel they have to explain or apologize for their physical identity, starting conversation with how they want to be considered (for example, "I may be a Moslem, but I abhor what the terrorists did in New York and Washington, D.C.," or " As the great grandchild of a former slave..."). The existing community members may well make assumptions about the newcomer's probable positions on issues, capabilities, and desirability for membership based on physical appearance or statements of self-identification.

Virtual communities "liberate the individual from the social constraints of embodied identity."[47] Participants have a choice as to how to identify themselves: through real or invented names, and, more importantly, on the substance of what they communicate. They have the opportunity to define for others the salient characteristics they want taken into account when others react to their communications. On line, people are who *they* say they are rather than who others say they are.

For those accustomed to judging and categorizing others first and listening to their arguments later, the power of taking on new identities is disconcerting and may simply be written off as deceit or duplicity. More importantly, the "right" to anonymously present oneself in any way undermines the component of democracy that makes one responsible for one's actions.

**Thinness of the Medium.** Face-to-face communications involve a large number of stimuli, audio, visual, spacial, etc. It is asserted that e-mail missiles or mouse clicks lack the depth and volume of interaction necessary for developing a true community. Among those with an opinion, 52% of Americans see the reduction of face-to-face communications as more of a danger than a benefit.[48] Proponents of virtual communities argue that the medium has the potential for richer interaction through presenting several different stimuli at once using text, pictures, video and sound. With advances in equipment, software and creative genius, such technology-supported messages could well rival traditional methods of communication. As Margolis and Resnick put it, "Chat rooms and other opportunities to interact with like-minded individuals do exist, but they are not central features of the most popular politically relevant Web sites. The Web can involve more participation on the part of the person online than can other media, but it is not the kind of active participation that is required of someone engaged in conversation....Although communication over the Internet still has the potential do democratize political discourse, in fact, it increasingly resembles the one-to-many pattern of broadcast media."[49]

**Depth of Emotional Involvement.** In traditional geographic communities, the expectation of long-term and unavoidable interaction stimulates many individuals to invest in maintaining community. Successes and failures of others in the community help develop a sense that "we are all in this together." The neighbor who lets his lawn go to weeds or who beautifully landscapes the median affects the land values of others. While one can try to avoid one's least-favored neighbors by timing one's comings and goings, the more common reaction is at a minimum to exchange greetings and look for ways to avoid conflict. The extreme action of physically departing from the geographic community is usually more of a penalty for the individual leaving than for the community itself.

Going to the mall is a lot like going on the Internet. Relationships are generally utilitarian. Shoppers seldom make friends with the proprietor, nor do they expect to exchange information with the sales clerk (who is likely to be a 17-year-old high school student) or fellow customers. While a contingent of teenage "mall rats" and senior citizen "mall walkers" attempt to re-create the town park or street corner in a climate-controlled setting, most shoppers are more intentional. They go to the mall for a particular set of items and plan their itinerary carefully, from which lot to park in to the order in which they will shop at various stores. Once inside they may do some "surfing," looking for sales or stopping into their favorite speciality shop.

Kraut et al. discuss the conception of strong and weak social ties in the context of the Internet. Strong ties are usually associated with physical proximity and "are the relationships that generally buffer people from life's stresses and that lead to better social and psychological outcomes." They posit that while the Internet may allow users to reach out and connect with others through e-mail and chat rooms, the relationships they create are relatively shallow and transitory. On-line friendships are likely to be more limited than face-to-face relationships. While individuals may be willing to exchange information over the Internet, it often lacks the passion necessary to convince others how to vote or to motivate them to take action in the political realm. On-line "netizens" may well have a larger pool of "right thinking" (that is, in agreement with them) casual acquaintances, but have few real friends who are confident enough in the relationship to disagree and who care enough to tell them that they are dead wrong. "By using the Internet, people are substituting poorer quality relationships for better relationships, that is, substituting weak ties for strong ones."[50]

Virtual communities allow one to exit and enter at will. "Relationships can be 'broken' at any stage by...simple withdrawal."[51] There is considerably less sense of social responsibility to others. It is hard to measure social attachment to communities in the geographic world, and even more difficult in the virtual world. Supporters of virtual community tend to rely on anecdotes and personal experience to explain—"I care about these people I meet through my computer."[52]

In the ease of entrance and exit from virtual communities lies the potential political consequence that individuals will find it easier to leave the community than to resolve conflicts. Politics is a process of resolving community conflicts in a way that satisfies participants enough so that the community survives. If virtual communities are little more than ephemeral sounding boards lacking any commitment to taking necessary collective action, they have the potential for skimming off some of the more rewarding political activities, such as expressing one's point of view, while relegating the rough choices to traditional community entities for which the virtual-community participant opts out when the really tough work has just begun.[53]

**Fragmentation and Insularity.** Face-to-face communities give residents less opportunity to choose with whom they will interact and with what information they will be confronted. Even the person living in the gated community of potentially like-minded demographic clones must venture out into the real world at some time and be confronted by individuals with wildly different lifestyles and perspectives. While no one can fully experience the full range of human existence, the day-to-day life of individuals in geographic communities provides, to the interested and discerning person, varying stimuli to hint at the rich mosaic of society.

Some selectivity is part of everyone's strategy to avoid information overload, but the appeal of virtual communities is the efficiency with which one can hone in to those information sources which relate to one's interests and are more likely to reinforce than challenge one's assumptions. In geographic communities, Rheingold, a proponent of virtual communities, points out that we, as individuals, "search through our pool of neighbors and professional colleagues, of acquaintances and acquaintances of acquaintances, in order to find people who share our values and interests. We then exchange information about one another, disclose and discuss our mutual interests, and sometimes we become friends. In a virtual community we can go directly to the place where our favorite subjects are being discussed, then get acquainted with people who share our passions....Your chances of making friends are magnified by orders of magnitude over the old methods of finding a peer group."[54]

Taking a more critical view, Van Alstyne and Brynjolfson assert that "Geography imposes an unavoidable heterogeneity. Adam Smith's butcher, brewer, and baker rubbed shoulders in a local town of physical neighbors. A virtual community of like-minded citizens, however, might be entirely homogeneous....As virtual citizens leave their physical neighborhoods behind, they inadvertently withdraw their contributions to their physical locales...,If individuals can choose their content, contacts and connections, then emphasizing preferred communities can balkanize interactions."[55]

Or as Anthony Wilhelm puts it, "Homophily—that is the propensity to gravitate to persons with similar viewpoints—is fairly common on the Internet, and to the extent that emerging communications networks allow individuals to more easily locate those with whom they agree, the notion of new communities is reified. Rather than creating environments in which ideas and viewpoints can be challenged and contested, the Internet may well be reinforcing and accelerating the pace of balkanization, a phenomenon that erodes deliberative democracy and the working out of problems and issues in the public sphere."[56]

David Shenk uses an analogy to argue that "Virtual communities resemble the semi-private spaces of modern health clubs more than the public spaces of agoras....Instead of meeting to discuss and debate issues of common concern to the society, members of these virtual communities met largely to promote their own interests and to reinforce their own like-mindedness....They...reinforce the fragmentation and factionalism of modern society...[and] instead of gathering us into a town square, the new information technology clusters us into social cubicles."[57]

Fernback and Thompson go even further arguing that "Virtual communities will be communities of interest rather than of geographical approximate or of historical or ethnic origin. As such, they will be further insulated from having to deal with the...workaday world....Instead of creating increasing cohesion, virtual communities are likely to have the opposite effect...so virtual communities can foster anomie. Instead of mass society leading to atomized individuals, however, it may be that it leads to atomized communities....Because virtual communities are likely to be private communities of interest, they will not readily or serendipitously be exposed to differing views that will help them and the large society grow and adapt to a changing world."[58]

The debate in this realm focuses on the diversity of viewpoints and the degree to which community-based conventional wisdom is challenged in geographic communities as opposed to virtual communities. Supporters of virtual communities argue that "Virtual communities may be insular, but no more or less insular than traditional communities."[59] The answer to this question is ultimately an empirical one.

**Increasing the Level of Conflict.** Politics involves forging societal compromises about competing values over which reasonable people disagree. While some conflict is inevitable, as proven by history, and desirable, as a spur to political action, there is a finite range of conflict necessary for a political entity to operate effectively. Both logic and initial research indicate that one cannot have the efficiency of finding one's narrow soul mates *and* the advantage of the broad range of competing information and perspectives necessary to discover realms and methods of compromise.

New technologies, at least as they are currently employed in politics, raise threats of more divisiveness, more lobbyists, more shrillness in the national discourse and less unity and cooperation. *Newsweek* talks about the emergence of special-interest "cybertribes," not based on race, gender, geography or their traditional cleavages, but on personal interest.[60] Former Speaker Thomas P. "Tip" O'Neill's pithy assertion that "All politics is local" now seems to need revision to state that "All politics is personal." "The splintering of cyberspace could be a polarizing pitfall rather than an opportunity to find creative new possibilities."[61]

Margolis and Resnick point out that "Whereas traditional democratic politics involves resolution of group conflict through combinations of pressures, bargaining, and compromise, some like-minded citizens of cyberspace may develop a type of civic life that involves little or no exchange among those who hold different opinions....Members of these virtual communities meet largely to promote their own interests...and to reinforce their own like-mindedness."[62]

While the new technologies *could* be used to build broader communities, expand informational horizons and facilitate compromise, there is no guarantee they will. A long view of history provides little assurance that new technologies will necessarily lead to more democratic outcomes. "By democratizing access to recorded information, the printing press set in motion the spread of literacy and education, literature and the arts, science and technology, and commerce and industry that led to the industrial revolution and the creation of democratic governments serving at the will of an informed populace."[63] Yet the printing press and later electronic technologies such as the telephone and radio "did not prevent new and even worse forms of autocracy from arising. Early on, these technologies contributed to the demise of the old monarchies and the broadening of popular participation in politics. But later, these same technologies were turned into tools of propaganda, surveillance and subjugation that enabled dictators to seize power and develop totalitarian regimes."[64] It is not so much what technology can do, but how it is used by both the senders and the receivers of information.

## How You Know Helps Determine What You Know

What you know depends to a large degree on the information access options you have, the options you choose to use, and the way you choose to use them. Increasingly, the recipient is in the information driver's seat making choices. It is an awesome opportunity. It is an awesome responsibility. It has awesome implications for both our personal lives and the nature of democracy in the future.

# Chapter 6
# What Do You Know?
# The Informed Citizen

> A popular government, without popular information, or the means of acquiring it, is but a Prologue to a Farce or Tragedy; or perhaps both. Knowledge will forever govern ignorance: Any people who mean to be their own Governors, must arm themselves with the power which knowledge gives.
> —James Madison, *The Writings of James Madison*

Democracy is the recurrent suspicion that over half the people are right over half the time. But being "right" assumes one knows the right questions, has a grasp of the full range of relevant answers, and has enough information to make a wise choice among the options. Information is to democracy as air is to fire—a necessary condition undergirding each of the above choices. Madison understood the importance of information and knowledge.[1]

## Who Knows What in the Cyber-Information Age?

All new information technologies begin with a demographically unrepresentative set of users. Their "arrival" as significant players in society comes with their ability to catch the fancy of a larger and more diverse set of users. Technologies unable to expand their user bases because of cost, skill requirements or lack of desired functionalities (such as CB radio, video disks, 8-track tapes, etc.) are doomed to the backwaters of information flow.

The population that inhabits the Internet and its various components is not a random sample of society. At a minimum, citizens hoping to tap new technology must surmount four hurdles. First, the technology must be *affordable*. Although prices of computers have declined and the cost of Internet access seems moderate to many, computers are an unaffordable luxury to a significant and non-random sample of the population.

Secondly, the technology must be *intellectually accessible*. Potential users need a certain amount of skill and need to overcome the psychological and intellectual conviction that the technology is beyond them. Improvement in this realm is progressing on two fronts. First, manufacturers and other vendors have increased the potential for off-the-shelf "plug and play" hardware and software, dramatically reducing the necessary technological skills and ameliorating the psychological barrier to usage. Also, in a modern application of the truism that "a little child shall lead them," each new generation arrives on the adult scene more familiar with the technology and less intimidated by it.

The third barrier is *time*. Time is a zero-sum game, with each activity competing against any other for attention. Flexibility of schedules and the absolute availability of time is not randomly distributed throughout the population. Unlike synchronous communication (face-to-face or telephone conversation), asynchronous communications via computer lessen the scheduling difficulty. Individuals can post inquiries and responses according to *their* schedule of availability.

Finally, in order to use the Web for political purposes, potential users must be *motivated*. Potential Web activists must overcome the basic barriers for all political participation, coming to the personal conclusion that political education and activity are worthwhile ("efficacy"—the sense that political involvement is an efficient use of one's time). They must also exhibit a preference on a political issue (even if that preference is only to develop a position). Finally, to turn to the Web for their activism, they must see it as a reliable and useful vehicle for gathering and/or communicating information.[2]

## The Demographics of the Net

The social character of the net is changing as levels of usage increase (see figure 6.1). Early on, Internet users were primarily male, wealthy, younger, and less likely to be members of minority groups. The demographics of the net have become more reflective of the general population as net usage has increased. In terms of attitudes, the Internet audience is also distinctive. They tend to be somewhat more liberal than the general population, especially on issues such as freedom of expression.[3]

### Figure 6.1. Internet Demographics

|  | All | Men | Women | Under 30 | Over 65 |
|---|---|---|---|---|---|
| Use of the Internet | 50% | 53% | 47% | 66% | 13% |
| Use of e-mail | 44% | 47% | 40% | 53% | 16% |
| On-line Access |  |  |  |  |  |
| w/in last year | 19% | 17% | 21% | 23% | 10% |
| 2-5 years | 28% | 30% | 25% | 45% | 7% |
| over 5 years | 6% | 8% | 3% | 6% | 1% |
| No access | 47% | 45% | 49% | 26% | 82% |

SOURCE: CBS News Poll of 1,165 adults, August 1999. Available at http//www.pollingreport.com/computer.htm.

The growth in reach and utilization of the Internet is dramatic. In 1995, only 9.4 million homes had access to the Internet. By 1999, that figure had increased to 45.2 million homes with an estimated 80 million residents.[4] Although today's Internet users are "still more affluent, educated and politically active than their fellow citizens, [they] resemble the general population more closely than did their predecessors. Like their predecessors, however, they use the Internet mostly for purposes other than learning about or participating in public and civic affairs."[5] As figure 6.2 shows, the Internet is the only growing source of political information.[6]

Internet users are a rich pool of potential political activists, bringing together the kinds of people who typically find politics interesting. "The Internet is really used as an extension of older, more common forms of media. It is not so much a different message they are seeking but a different method of delivery." Far from turning their backs on traditional media, heavy Internet users are actually more likely to read a daily newspaper and just as likely as the general public to get news from television.[7]

**Figure 6.2. Source of Presidential Campaign News**

|      | Television | Newspapers | Radio | Magazines | Internet |
|------|------------|------------|-------|-----------|----------|
| 1992 | 84%        | 53%        | 17%   | 6%        | N.A.     |
| 1996 | 78%        | 46%        | 18%   | 6%        | 2%       |
| 2000 | 71%        | 29%        | 13%   | 2%        | 6%       |

NOTE: Percentages are averages for multiple polls taken in each election.

SOURCE: Pew Research Center for the People and the Press, fall 2000 survey of 8,378 adults. Available at http//www.people-press.org/questionnaires.online00que.htm.

## When Do We Know What We Know?

Timing is critical in politics. Knowing something too early, and especially too late, makes the information effectively meaningless. The potential recipients of information must be receptive, which involves convincing them that the information available is important to have. If information arrives before the need is perceived, the reaction is most likely, "That's nice, but let me get on to something interesting." Purveyors of information spend much of their time trying to convince potential audiences of relevance. If the initial grounding in relevance has not been plowed, the "seeded" information will lie fallow.

On the other hand, much political information is time sensitive since its relevance depends on its utility in helping an individual make a decision. Finding out damaging (or supporting) information about a candidate a few days after the election may increase frustration or smug satisfaction, but does nothing to help the individual when entering the voting booth.

A key characteristic of cyber-information is the irrelevance of distance and the instantaneous nature of delivery. Corrections come almost simultaneously with the initial messages. In political campaigns charges and counter-charges fly without having to wait for printing presses or film editing. In fact, with e-mail messages posted on the screen with the latest first, one might get the corrected version or reaction *before* the original message. We have all received the disconcerting "disregard previous message" communication before receiving the previous message. Most of us, however, rush to find out what we are supposed to disregard.

Increasing the pace of politics—and life in general—has consequences. Some people fall by the wayside, unable to handle the rush of stimuli. We increasingly live in a world of "tentative conclusions" rather than "abiding certainties." What we believe today can be washed over by the next wave of contradictory information. While the "onion peel" theory of attitude formation, which argues that what we learn early has the strongest effect on our later opinions, may well have some validity for determining our interests and helping us evaluate sources, the lure of new information with the patina of immediacy and the enhancements of an appealing format increasingly overwhelms our outlooks. The "shelf life" of opinions and the information they are based on are considerably shorter in the contemporary era. For example, the popularity of President George W. Bush and Congress increased over 30 percentage points after the terrorist attacks in New York and Washington, D.C. The public's trust in government shot up to new records. This is not an isolated example. Similar dramatic shifts accompanied President Kennedy's initiatives during the Cuban missile crisis and the aborted invasion at the Bay of Pigs. In fact dramatic presidential action almost invariably improves the president's popularity, regardless of whether that action ultimately proves to be wise or foolish.

The maintenance of high levels of trust and support is another thing. After the glow of dramatic action, political institutions and office holders drop back to more "normal" levels of support.

Existing and emerging technologies arrive without a set of established norms and expectations. As discussed in chapter 4, the ease and speed of hurling e-mails back and forth led to significant "flaming," the sending of intemperate responses. The seeming anonymity of responding via e-mail removes much of the sensitivity to the views of others that we have learned to show in face-to-face communications. The speed of typing a response on the screen as opposed to the more onerous task of writing a letter seems to lead to seeing e-mail as a less permanent record for which the writer holds little responsibility. E-mailers take less time framing and composing messages in ways that would avoid offense. The bottom line leads people to say things in e-mails they would never say in person or in a letter.

## When We Think We Know

New technologies lend the patina of truth to preposterous pronouncements. Urban legends emerge, spread like a hydra-headed monster, and seldom fully die even when proven to be entirely false. Shortly after the September 11, 2001, terrorist attacks, an e-mail spread around the country arguing that a respected researcher had evidence that CNN had used 1991 pictures of Palestinians celebrating to illustrate a story about Palestinian support for the current attack. In reality, the CNN pictures were legitimate.[8] The e-mail turned out to be a hoax, but our distrust of the media led to its initial acceptance. About the same time, Rush Limbaugh promoted an e-mail asserting the Canadian-born ABC anchor Peter Jennings had criticized President Bush for not returning to the White House. The publicity included Jennings' e-mail address and telephone numbers, and the public outcry shut down his e-mail and filled his answering machines with vitriolic attack. In reality, Jennings had never made such a statement, but the opportunity to lash out at a "foreigner criticizing the good old U.S.A."

was too tempting for many. Limbaugh later recanted the story, but not before it was well implanted in the minds of many.[9]

There is a natural tendency to seek and believe stories that fit our preconceptions. Often those preconceptions have been built by the media looking for simple stories that can be presented in 90 seconds or less. During the early 1990s, one common story line was George Herbert Walker Bush's isolation from the real word. On the surface, many people felt that anyone with four names could not really understand what life was like for the average person. His "sins" were exacerbated by his long career as a government employee—a suspect class of workers in the eyes of many. Thus, stories of Bush being out of touch began with an instant patina of legitimacy. The public was quick to accept a story of Bush being baffled by a grocery checkout scanner, a technology most Americans had learned to accept. *The New York Times* ran a headline, "Bush Encounters the Supermarket, Amazed." LEXIS-NEXIS lists over fifty print and TV stories about Bush's amazement, with few indicating that the implication of Bush being out of touch was a stretch. In reality, the thrust of the story was false. Bush had shown amazement, but it was over a newer cutting-edge scanning technology that would have amazed most citizens. Many of the TV stories showed stock footage of traditional scanners or a picture of Bush in front of a scanner similar to the ones most shoppers encountered every day. By not putting the story in proper context, Bush came off as an elitist, clearly too disengaged from everyday life to be president of the people. Only a few newspapers corrected the initial error. The damage was done and many credited his loss of the 1992 election to his image of being out of touch with ordinary Americans.[10]

Bill Clinton also lost support due to a believable but largely false story line. Clinton had become marked as a spoiled child of the 1960s, as manifested in his self-indulgence of fast foods and the perks of office. A story emerged that he had disrupted flights from the Los Angeles airport to allow a hairstylist to the Hollywood stars, Cristophe, to give him a haircut on the runway. In reality, only one unscheduled flight was delayed for two minutes,[11] but the story had already become a legend. The 23 stories listed by LEXIS-NEXIS prominently focused on Clinton's lack of consideration for others.

The speed of new technologies allows misinformation to spread at tremendous rates over large distances. Just as deep space lacks the life-sustaining chemical element oxygen, in cyberspace it is harder to step back and take a deep breath of truth-sustaining information. The speed, volume and impressive presentation of cyber-information can cloud the truth just as easily as it can reveal it.

---

**Figure 6.3. Media Trust of Campaign Information**

|  | Print Media | Television | Internet Sites |
|---|---|---|---|
| **Evaluation of Each Medium** | | | |
| % "fair and unbiased" * | 38 | 53 | 48 |
| % with an opinion on fairness | 49 | 71 | 32 |

NOTE: Respondents were asked to evaluate specific sources relative to their coverage of the 2000 presidential election campaign. Print media included *USA Today* (most trusted), *New York Times, Los Angeles Times* (least trusted), *Time* and *Newsweek*. Television included CNN (most trusted), CBS, NBC, FOX, and ABC (least trusted). Internet sites included YAHOO (most trusted), MSN, CNN, and MSNBC (least trusted).

* % of those with an opinion.

SOURCE: Rasmussen Research poll of 2,250 "likely voters," July 2000. Available at *http://www.portraitofamerica.com/html/poll-1462.html*.

---

We, as an information audience, trust televison more than we trust print, even though the development of printed information requires more time for thoughtful consideration and involves more screening. When asked to compare which source they would trust if confronted with competing stories, 51% of American adults with an opinion chose television; 25%, newspapers; 9%, radio; and 6%, magazines.[12] During a political campaign, likely voters trust the Internet about as much as they trust television, although fewer voters have an opinion about established Internet sites (see figure 6.3). Going beyond the established sites, much of the information on the Internet was created with little time for thoughtful consideration and is much less likely to be passed through the corrective screens of fact checkers and editors. In a recent poll, 41% of adults with an opinion trusted information from the Internet "completely" or "quite a lot." Only 15% did not trust it at all.[13]

## Who Controls What We Know?

The shift from broadcast television to the cable era was seen as broadening the scope of information providers by lowering the entrance costs. The increased news hole on a variety of competing cable networks increased the potential for committed individuals and organizations to insert their message into the political dialogue. If free media was not forthcoming, the lower advertising costs on cable and the time set aside for public-access programming allowed an alternative low-cost venue. The Internet was seen as another vehicle for proving the "empowerment thesis," asserting that new technologies reduce the power of existing political institutions to the benefit of new interests and causes.[14]

One of the more consistent predictions was that politics on the Internet would see the flowering of new parties and interest groups that would challenge the dominance of the Republican and Democratic parties and the existing key interest-group players.[15] Robert Dahl argued that "Telecommunications can give every citizen the opportunity to place questions of their own on the public agenda and participate in discussions with experts, policy makers and fellow citizens."[16]

While the evidence is not completely one-sided, proponents of the "reinforcement thesis" make a strong case that new technologies are more easily captured for use by existing power holders than by newcomers with competing political agendas. They conclude that "Politics on the Internet is politics as usual conducted mostly by familiar parties, candidates, interest groups, and news media."[17] While the Internet with its relatively low cost of entry has the *potential* for evening the political playing field and countering existing elite domination of politics, there is little evidence of this happening. "The access of marginal movements to a new and powerful medium of mass communication has not led them to make significant headway into the real world. The problem lies more in the message than in the medium....Those who have been powerful in the past—established organizations, the wealthy, and the privileged—are moving into cyberspace and taking their advantage with them."[18] The new technologies tend to "amplify the voice of those who are already active."[19]

To the degree that the information transferred is based on choices by editors or moderators, the range of views expressed is limited. After an empirical analysis of who is handed the microphone on commercial and public television news, Croteau and Hoynes conclude that "contemporary televison news lacks...sustained diversity." The "usual cast of talking-head characters" allowed to express themselves are decidedly middle-of-the-road, with editors and producers lopping off the extremes on both ends.[20] While Internet providers and e-mail list moderators are less efficient and more hesitant to censor, some participants find that free speech on the Net still comes with some limits.

Even lower production and distribution costs can more easily be absorbed by mainstream political parties, interest groups and commercial entities. Once they saw their audiences shift to cable, the major television networks shifted some of their efforts in that direction, creating outlets such as MSNBC. Taking the position "If you can't fight them, join them," existing media created their own sophisticated Web sites, luring surfers with unique information while touting their more traditional televised or print vehicles. Even the most cursory scan of political Web sites indicates that organizations with more resources are able to develop more complex, multi-functional and compelling sites. Since most visitors first gain access through search engines, political activist groups can pay to have their sites show up first or purchase banner advertising to lure visitors. Once a visitor is at their site, organizations with greater resources can increase the likelihood of future visits with constant updating and/or the use of "cookies," marking one's visit and generating later messages inviting the user back.

## Who Cares About Politics in Cyberspace?

Proponents of cyberdemocracy see the public thirsting for new, more timely and better political information, ready to pounce and take action.[21] Others are less sanguine, arguing that the Internet will "flood users with so much information that it will become impossible to sort the legitimate from the illegitimate, the good from the bad, and the accurate from the inaccurate."[22]

Shenk questions the public's interest in greater political information, and arguing that pure democracy facilitated by greater information is both unworkable and dangerous, saying that "the electronic town hall allows for speedy communication and bad decision-making." He concludes that most people choose to be ignorant about politics because they don't see it as relevant or important.[23]

While it is clear the Internet provides the ability to find expanded, better and more timely information about civic and political affairs, there is no assurance that availability necessarily leads to increased utilization. While an "If you build it, they will come" outlook makes a good Hollywood story, it seldom matches reality.[24] "The average citizen's relatively low demand for information about [political] affairs, coupled with the imperatives of the market, tend to discourage efforts to devote larger proportions of the media's limited resources to these matters....Why should we expect that the most prominent sources of information about political and civic affairs on the Internet should be much different from those already found in other mass media?"[25]

The information choices and demographics of on line users do not yet bode well for the use of the Internet as a significant tool for politics. In the 2000 election, only 19% of adults reported receiving any news about the election on the Internet, although that figure was up from 7% in 1996.[26] Research on the preferences indicates that Web surfers seek news about science, health and technology more frequently than about political and civic affairs. When they do focus on politics, their interests lead them more to local than national or international affairs.[27] Utilizing one's limited time to gather information on line could well *reduce* the amount of political information one might be exposed to as opposed to leaving the choice of content up to broadcast media. A "Gresham's Law"[28] of information might exist. Easy access to sports and entertainment information crowds out of political information (see figure 6.4).

### Figure 6.4. Preferred Internet Sites

**Content of Sites for Which Respondents Report Going on Line**

| | |
|---|---|
| Weather | 64% |
| Technology news | 59% |
| Business news | 58% |
| Entertainment | 58% |
| Sports | 47% |
| International news | 47% |
| Health news | 46% |
| Political news | 43% |

SOURCE: PEW Research Center for the People and the Press national sample of 3,184 adults, December 1998. Available at http//www.people-press.org/questionnaires/tech98que.htm

To some degree the problem is one of too much information coming at us too fast. Twenty-eight percent of Americans feel overloaded by the rich information environment in which they live, while 62% like having so much information available.[29] Getting up to speed on a new area of inquiry leads to almost impossible updating of a mountain of information. We were once limited to our own personal libraries, the limited holdings of nearby public libraries and the information we could gain from face-to-face conversations with friends and associates.

In an era of more limited information, personal research was guided by the goal of *closure*. Once our sources began to repeat the same information, we felt we had mastered the field. There are fewer and fewer realms of research where closure is likely. Each new source leads us to a dozen new sources in the form of mentions in the text, formal citations or Web links. There tends to be a growing attitude that "If I can't master it all, why master any of it?" We manage the abundance beast by being increasingly more selective. In Shenk's words, "At a certain level of input, the law of diminishing returns takes effect; the glut of information no longer adds to our quality of life, but instead begins to cultivate stress, confusion and even ignorance....Data smog gets in the way; it crowds out quiet moments, and obstructs much-needed contemplation....We face a paradox of abundance-induced amnesia....The more we know, the less we know. The vicious spiral drives a growing wedge between people within different spheres of knowledge."[30]

"Because the Internet provides instant and almost cost-free information, it should enable the ordinary citizen to be fully informed about all relevant policy areas." The limitation in its potential for creating a more informed citizenry lies more in public motivations than in technological feasibility. "The Net is now and will continue to be a boon to those who already have an active and sustained interest in public affairs, but there is little evidence that the Internet by itself will increase the attentive public."[31] For most citizens, neither convenience, low cost nor flashy presentation will lure them toward gathering information about topics in which they have little inherent interest. Besides, since it is so easy to spread false information, there is a temptation to throw up one's hands and exclaim, "What am I supposed to believe?"

Before simply concluding that the Internet is irrelevant to the process of informing political outlooks, two caveats are important. Current utilization patterns do not necessarily predict the future. It is possible that the potential of the Internet for informing the public still lies ahead. The record of other facilitating technologies such as radio and television indicate that technology alone will clearly not be the causal factor. Secondly, *who* turns to the Internet for political information may be more important than *what* is available. As political activist Ed Schwartz points out, "Why should people who hate politics on television try to find it on the World Wide Web....The aim [of Web users in politics] is not to reach the people least interested in politics, but the most committed—activists who will go door-to-door with fliers and registration cards and information about the campaigns."[32] The technology may be an efficient method of informing the already motivated and interested without having much spillover effect on the broader population. The fact that those who are politically information-rich now have an efficient tool to get even richer is not an insignificant outcome.

## Technology-induced Empowerment?

There is little evidence that Madison's desire for a politically informed public has arrived through the application of modern technology much more than was the case when information was passed from mouth to mouth over the cracker barrel. *Some* citizens have more information (and possibly misinformation) about more specific realms and have it faster than ever before. To some degree the new inequalities in information access are self-imposed as individuals take advantages of the choices new technologies provide. For those uninterested in politics, the new technologies may actually reduce their exposure to political information. Although the technologies have some empowerment potential, their utilization largely reinforces existing power holders and entrenches the outlooks they prefer.

# Chapter 7
# The Where, What and How of Politics in the Cyberdemocracy Age

Democracy is not a spectator sport. Among all the potential characteristics defining a democracy (basic rights, access to information, receptive public officials, etc.) the holy grail remains civic participation. Unless citizens actually participate in meaningful ways to affect the personnel and policies of government, all the rights, resources and receptivity mean little. While we sometimes hear a feeble echo that "people aren't participating because things are going so well," concerns over declining rates of voting and other modes of political participation are deafening. Despite rising levels of education, a more equitable distribution of opportunities, and increased access to information—all purported correlates of expanded participation—it is hard to find a measure of political activity that has increased. Its seems like an example of the old Pennsylvania Dutch tourist sign, "The hurrieder I go the behinder I get." That task at hand is to determine some of the causes of this decline in political participation in the context of changing social patterns and technological innovations. To what degree do the changes contribute to or help ameliorate the seeming freefall in political engagement?

## Where You Sit Determines If You Sit: Modern Political Geography

On the surface it makes sense that physically rootless people have more trouble establishing the social anchoring that facilitates both motivation and resources to participate in politics. Previous research indicates that physically mobile citizens were significantly less likely to vote in national elections even when demographic variables and voter registration laws were held constant.[1]

The impact of residential mobility on political participation varies with the type of election. For presidential elections, information costs are lower and the perceived stake is greater for all voters. Personal identification with the outcome varies less with geographic location for presidential elections than for congressional elections. In the 2000 election, long-term (over 20 years) residents were twice as likely to pay attention to the presidential campaign and three times as likely to pay attention to the congressional campaign as compared with short term (under 2 years) residents (see figure 7.1).[2]

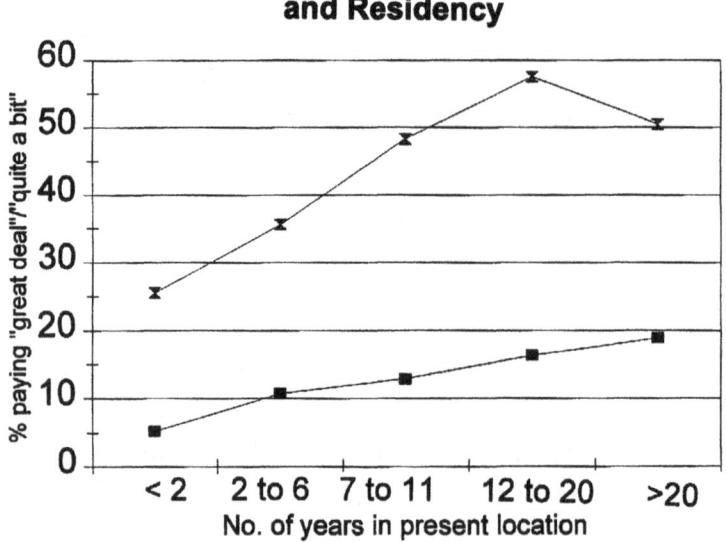

Figure 7.1. Attention Paid to Campaign and Residency

SOURCE: 2000 National Election Study (#3131) conducted by the Institute for Social Research at the University of Michigan.

Voting requires both interest and the ability to fulfill residency requirements. Previous research has shown that long-term residents (over 10 years) are 23% more likely to vote in midterm elections, but only 10.7% more likely to participate in presidential elections than those who have moved to the community within one year of the election. In recent presidential elections, long-term residents were significantly more likely to participate than short-term residents (see figure 7.2). This pattern maintains, even when one controls for other correlates of participation such as education and income. The slight decline in participation by the longest-term residents reflects the fact that this pool of potential voters includes a large number of older voters who often find it more difficult to get to the polls.

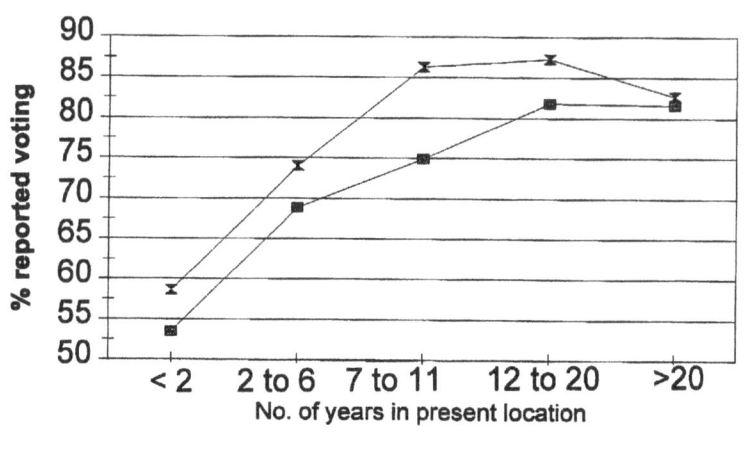

**Figure 7.2. Voting Participation and Residency**

SOURCE: 2000 National Election Study (#3131) conducted by the Institute for Social Research at the University of Michigan

In terms of other modes of participation, smaller but consistent differences appear between long- and short-term residents when it comes to working for candidates, talking about politics or trying to convince others how to vote in midterm elections, with fewer differences in presidential election behavior.[3]

The impact of physical mobility on political participation is likely to be more evident for local participation alternatives. Uprooted individuals and those living in communities of limited commitment may not experience a reduced interest in national events; in fact, they may be drawn toward them to fill the void in concern over local politics. Similarly, uprooted individuals will not necessarily encounter the increased information costs for keeping abreast of national politics as they would for local politics. The uprooted citizenry hypothesis is consistent with the dramatic decline of local political party organizations and local voting.

Not all of the differences in participation associated with residential mobility depend on motivational factors. Political parties, candidates and interest groups target long-term residents both out of convenience and strategy. Long-term residents are more likely to appear on established membership, publication and voting registration lists. Being well-connected socially, they are also better placed to pass along mobilization messages. Given limited resources, those with an interest in mobilization will also focus their efforts on the most participatory segments of their potentially supportive populations. Previous research has shown that long-term residents are 7% more likely to be contacted by political parties than are new residents.[4] In the 2000 election campaign, the parties were almost twice as likely to send long-term residents literature through the mail, while long-term residents were almost three times more likely to remember having been contacted by party workers (see figure 7.3).

It is widely assumed that owning a home "increases one's stake in the established system and gives citizens a strong financial incentive to participate" in the political process.[5] Previous survey data bears this out for voting, with over 90% of home owners indicating a high likelihood of voting, compared with 83% of renters.[6] In the 2000 election, 84% of home owners reported having voted, compared with 59% of renters. Home owners also pay more attention to the campaign, with 50% paying attention to the presidential campaign (compared with 39% of renters) and 14% paying attention to the congressional campaign (compared with 10% of renters). It could be that differentials in political interest and activity actually result from the demographics of owners and renters. Renters, as opposed to owners, are more likely to be younger, poorer and less educated individuals, yet the lack of permanency associated with renting remains as an independent influence on political interest and activity. The oldest renters, however, are slightly more likely to pay attention to congressional elections than compatriots their age who own their own homes.

**Figure 7.3. Party Contact and Residency**

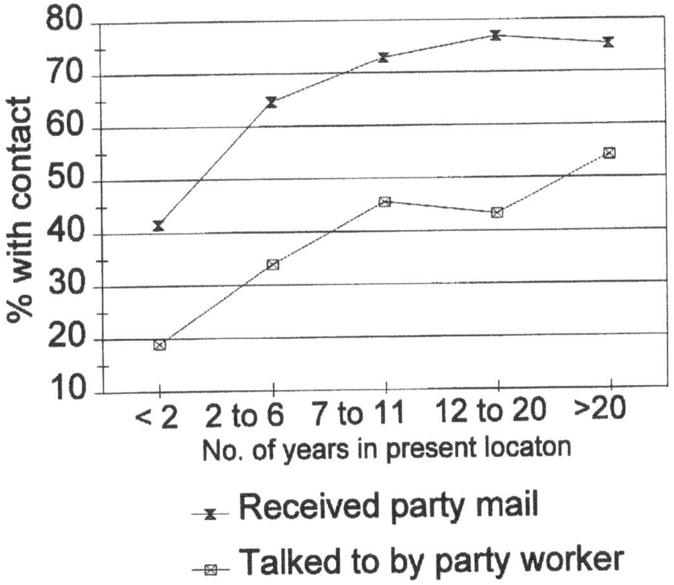

—x— Received party mail
—▭— Talked to by party worker

SOURCE: 2000 National Election Study (#3131) conducted by the Institute for Social Research at the University of Michigan.

Physical mobility clearly affects voter turnout. One detailed analysis of off-year (non-presidential) elections revealed that even after holding standard demographic variables constant, individuals living in a community for less than 2 years were over 20% less likely to vote than those who had lived in the same community for over 10 years. Individuals living in a community for 3 to 5 years were 9% less likely to vote than those having lived there for over 10 years, while those living in the community for 6 to 9 years, were only 1% less likely to vote than those with 10 or more years of permanent residence. The analysis also indicates that the drop-off in voting associated with mobility is greater among wealthier and better-educated voters. This counter-intuitive finding is probably best explained by the differing types of moves associated with each group of voters. Low-income and less-educated voters are more likely to be subjects of local moves, while better-educated and wealthier voters find themselves subjected to the much more disruptive long-distance moves across state lines.[7]

Simply looking at the level of participation of the more mobile segments of the population may not tell the whole story. Not all groups in the population choose or are forced into physical mobility as a way of life. Younger citizens inherently have less time to have remained in a location and often must move to complete their education and/or begin their careers. Residential mobility clearly declines with age. Whereas 22.6% of adults under 30 in 2000 had lived in their current community for less than 2 years, that was true of only 2.6% of people in their 60s and less than 1% of those over 60. On the other end of the mobility scale, 27.2% of younger voters (under 30) had lived in their community for over 20 years; that figure increased to 36% for those in their 40s and 68% for those in their 60s.[8]

Corporations move better-educated and more skillful employees in their organization and often reward those willing to move with greater salary increases. Fifty-seven percent of adults with less than a high school education have lived in their communities for over 20 years, compared with 36% of college graduates. The pattern for income is similar, with 48% of those with incomes under $15,000 having been in the community over 20 years, compared with 37% of those with incomes over $75,000.

To the degree that mobility is related to greater income and education, rootlessness competes with the tendencies of people from such groups to participate in politics more. On the other hand, younger citizens are forced into more mobility, which may exacerbate their traditionally lower participation rates. Previous research shows that the higher education level of frequent long-distance movers pulls them in two directions in terms of participation. Better-educated individuals are seemingly less hindered by mobility than those potential voters with lower levels of education who generally participate at lower rates.[9] The question is whether residential mobility exerts an independent influence on political participation or whether it simply reflects the demographics of frequent movers.

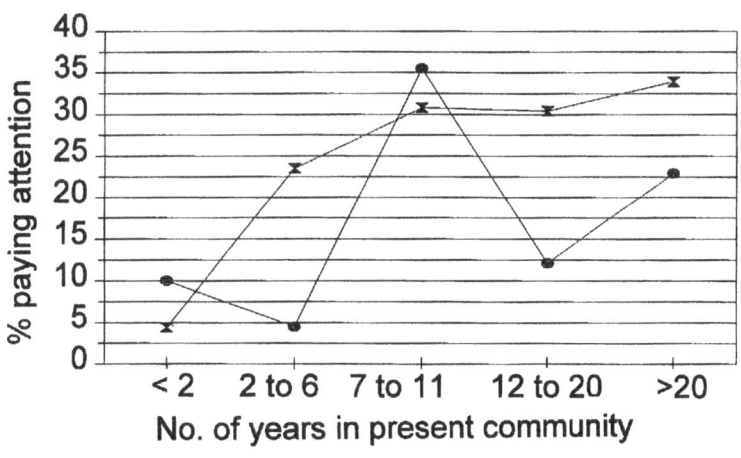

**Figure 7.4. Attention Paid to Congressional Campaign by Education and Residency**

SOURCE: 2000 National Election Study (#3131) conducted by the Institute for Social Research at the University of Michigan.

A key test would be to look at interest in more local elections where the information costs are higher and perceived citizen impact is lower. By controlling for other variables it is possible to assess the independent impact of residential mobility. Education is a clear correlate of political interest and participation. Figure 7.4 shows that despite the fact that more highly educated individuals pay more attention to congressional campaigns, greater mobility tends to dampen the interest of both the more and less educated in the population. A similar, but significantly muted pattern is evident for interest in the presidential campaign and voting in presidential election years. A comparable pattern is evident for income. Like education, income tends to correlate with political interest and political participation. As figure 7.5 indicates, while wealthier individuals are somewhat more likely to show an interest in congressional campaigns, residential mobility reduces the interest level at every income level. As with education, similar but muted influences are evident for voter attentiveness and voting in presidential elections.

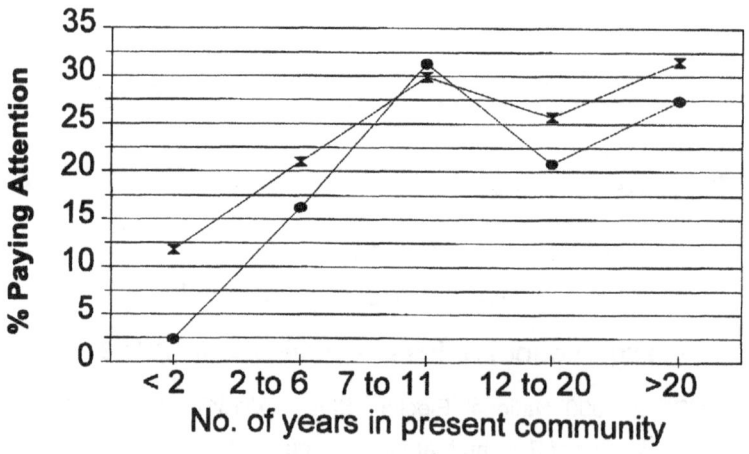

**Figure 7.5. Attention Paid to Congressional Campaign by Income and Residency**

SOURCE: 2000 National Election Study (#3131) conducted by the Institute for Social Research at the University of Michigan.

A key test of the independent impact of residential mobility relates to age. Younger citizens are both more residentially mobile and less interested in politics. A key question is whether their low level of involvement is associated with age factors per se or whether residential mobility exerts an independent influence. As figure 7.6 reveals, residential mobility depresses political interest among all voters regardless of age. As with the other variables, the impact is also evident but less clear for interest in presidential campaigns and the act of voting itself.

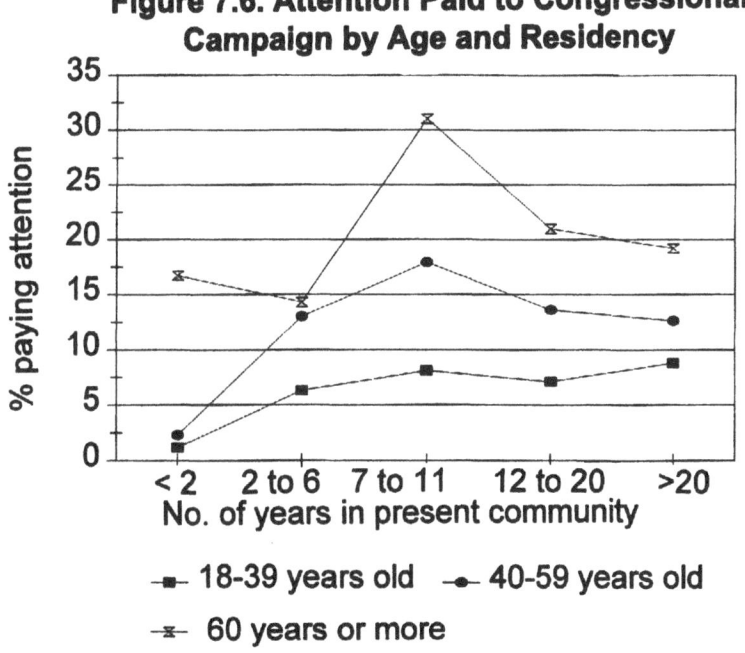

Figure 7.6. Attention Paid to Congressional Campaign by Age and Residency

—■— 18-39 years old   —●— 40-59 years old
—✕— 60 years or more

SOURCE: 2000 National Election Study (#3131) conducted by the Institute for Social Research at the University of Michigan.

The bottom line is clear. Residential mobility works against political interest and involvement even when one takes into account the key variables typically associated with interest and participation. Individuals with more limited tenure in a community are not a random sample of the population in terms of age, education and income, but it is not their uniqueness on these variables that fully accounts for their lack of political engagement. Being out of the political information loop along with the legal impediments to engagement associated with voter registration laws and the attitude that political involvement is not viable if one is unaware of the issues and their historical impact on the community—all threaten participation. Each of these potential culprits in depressing political involvement is directly related to residential mobility and is likely to increase as mobility becomes more common.

## Information and Political Action: To Know Is to Act

Sorting out cause and effect is often difficult when dealing with the complexities of human behavior. Proponents of various technologies like to point out that their users are "some of the most politically active of all citizens." The problem is that users of new technologies generally over represent better-educated and more financially secure individuals, precisely the kind of people who are more likely to participate at higher levels anyway. The more important question is whether using new information technologies accelerates differences in participation or depresses them.

On the surface, the political interest and activity of Internet users seems obvious, but much of the increased political proclivity stems from the unique demographics of those using the Internet. Internet users are younger, better educated and wealthier than the population as a whole. Increased education and income have long been strong predictors of higher political interest and activity. As figures 7.7 and 7.8 indicate, interest in congressional campaigns is less for Internet users among most educational and income groupings. Internet access seemingly depresses interest most among the least well educated and the least financially secure. The pattern is less clear and less dramatic in terms of attention paid to presidential campaigns, with non-Internet users surpassing Internet users in the majority of categories. The evidence points to Internet use as a distraction from political activity, especially when it comes to attention paid to more local congressional races. The impact of Internet use on actual voting in 2000 indicates that users showed a decreased propensity to vote, based on what one would expect by their demographics.

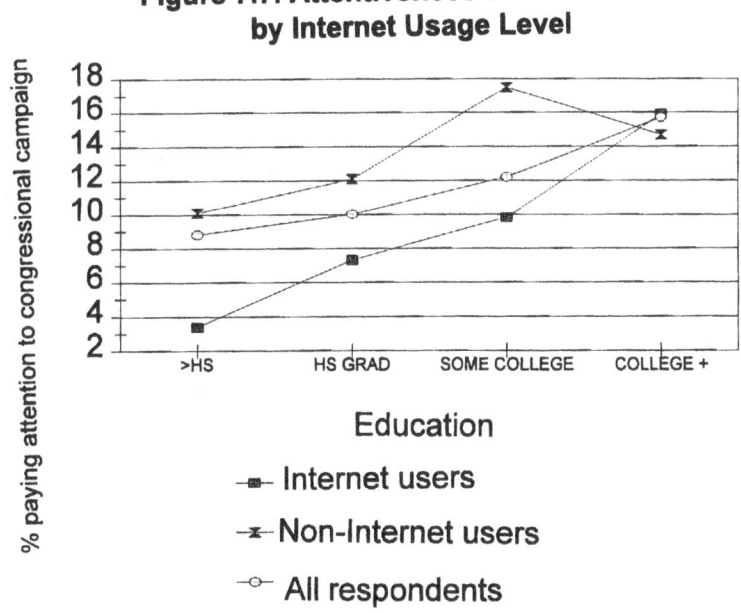

Figure 7.7. Attentiveness and Education by Internet Usage Level

SOURCE: 2000 National Election Study (#3131) conducted by the Institute for Social Research at the University of Michigan.

The aggregate higher level of political interest and involvement of Internet users stems from the demographic imbalance of so many Internet users in the higher education and income groups who participate at high levels *despite* the Internet "distraction." Overall figures mask the fact that except for the higher education and income groups, Internet users are particularly less likely to attune to more local political battles. At best, Internet usage draws potential voters toward national concerns; at worst, it pulls them away from political involvement in general.

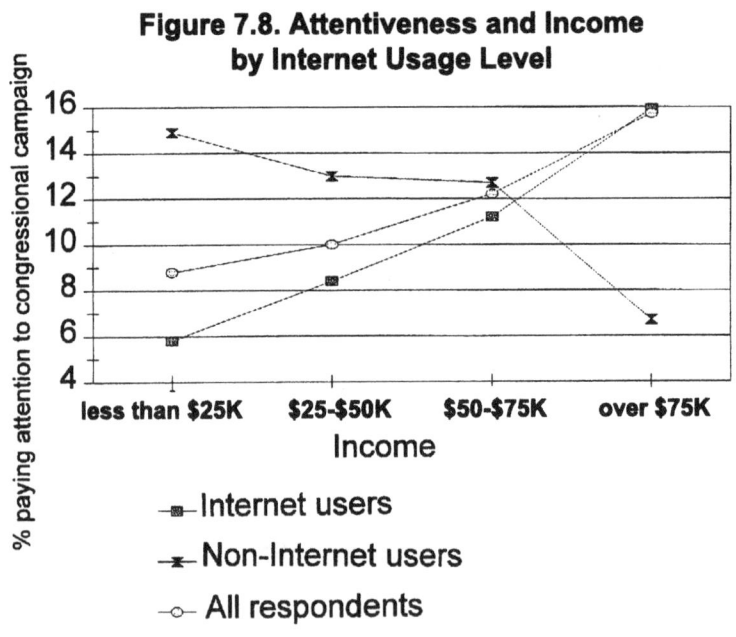

Figure 7.8. Attentiveness and Income by Internet Usage Level

SOURCE: 2000 National Election Study (#3131) conducted by the Institute for Social Research at the University of Michigan.

## It Takes Two to Techno: Political Institutions Face the Wandering Techno Tribes

Geographically mobile individuals skilled in the use of geography-disregarding technologies, such as computers, face difficulty when trying to activate public officials whose legal duties and political experience tie them to established geographical constituencies.

Politics is so risky that its denizens seek safety in whatever routines and patterns they can find. Most politicians are strategically conservative, assuming that if a route to position and power worked in the past, it is likely to work in the future. New approaches, if embraced at all, are embraced as add-ons to supplement old approaches.

### The Technology Promise

> Politics and government will be transformed by free communications, changing the balance of power between governments and their citizens. People will become better informed and will be able to communicate their views to their government's leaders and representatives more easily. Politicians will become more sensitive to lobbying and to public-opinion polls.
> —Frances Cairncross, *The Death of Distance*

Proponents of cyberdemocracy paint a rosy picture of a more equal and inclusive politics that "expands the range of partnerships available to us and enables us to work together on behalf of common goals."[10] They see the new technologies as increasing the quality of public debate and policy making by supporting, "all three parts of the political process: gathering information, public discussion and debate to consensus, and taking action. A sustained dialogue is possible online that is simply impossible at a meeting or hearing, where there is less time to ponder and digest the words that literally dissipate into thin air....The information and points generated by an online discussion can remain available for all to review....The quality of the discussion is at a higher level, because people think more about what they are going to say. Many assertions that are factually wrong that might slide by at a meeting get nailed online, where readers have the time and resources to check facts. Everyone can have a say before it is all said and done, whereas at a meeting or a hearing, time and place impose constraints on discussion and require rationing of the time allocated to each person."[11]

The promise is appealing but lacks any consistent evidence of broad-based positive outcomes in the real world.[12] Proponents argue that "time will tell." In the meantime, the more skeptical point out inherent impediments and potential dangers.

## The Cold Realities

"A new technology is opening up new vistas for democracy, education and personal enrichment, a magazine predicts. 'The government,' it says, 'will be a living thing to its citizens instead of an abstract and unseen force....Elected representatives will not be able to evade their responsibility to those who put them in office....The new medium will be like a gigantic school...and have a greater student body than all our universities put together.' The year was 1922, radio was the new technology, and the magazine was *Radio Broadcast.*"[13]

Be wary of reformers bearing gifts. Proponents of change typically oversell the advantages and undersell the limitations and dangers. The skeptics of cyberdemocracy point out limitations in the kinds of communities technologies facilitate, the need to clearly define the nature of democracy one wishes to pursue, and the confusion over causes and effects.

### The Organizational Underpinnings of Democracy. 
Alexis de Tocqueville's conception of America as a "nation of joiners" brought forth an image of face-to-face communications over cracker barrels, in social clubs and at union halls. Like-minded (and often demographically similar)

individuals would join together to share ideas and in some cases use the power and resources of numbers to put pressure on government. The old-line interest groups were largely bottom-up operations, with national organizations and professional staffs emerging to serve the needs of state and local units.

Many of the most powerful advocacy organizations on the contemporary scene emerged from the center as opposed to bubbling up from the grassroots membership at the bottom. Interest-group entrepreneurs took advantage of "patron grants [from foundations or wealthy individuals], direct mail techniques, and the capacity to convey images and messages through the mass media [that] have changed the realities of organization building and maintenance."[14] These cause-oriented advocacy groups, such as Common Cause, Children's Defense Fund and American Association of Retired People, "offer busy, privileged Americans a rich menu of opportunities to, in effect, hire other professionals and managers to represent their values and interests in public life."[15] While these are efficient models for applying new media and communications technologies, such groups lack meaningful opportunities for members to influence their agendas and are heavily tilted toward the goals and interests of upper-middle-class individuals with the skills, resources and motivations such groups target. In many cases "membership" involves little more than writing a check, often motivated by non-policy-oriented selective benefits such as prescription drug discounts, magazine subscriptions, and other preferments not offered to non-members. The professional lobbyists then encourage decision-makers to make the inferential leap that checkbook membership implies support of the centrally directed policy preferences and that they speak for "xx million concerned Americans."

The term "virtual community" may well imply more than what really happens when individuals communicate on line. Communications are not enough evidence to suggest an actual community. Communities require (1) a minimum level of interactivity; (2) a variety of commentators; (3) a minimum level of sustained membership; and (4) a virtual common public space where a significant portion of interactive computer-mediated communications occur.[16] A community requires more than broadcasting information, even to an identifiable group. A significant portion of the recipients must publicly respond and contribute to forming and refining the group's collective purpose. To be relevant in the political sphere, virtual communities must take some action in support of refining and guiding public policy.

While technology has the potential for expanding the pool of those who are politically involved, it has yet to reach that goal. The less educated and less financially secure are relatively unfruitful targets for technology-based interest-group entrepreneurs. Such individuals are less likely to be "connected" through traditional or e-mail lists, which serve as the basis for stimulating membership, and, even if contacted, they are less likely to exhibit a willingness to part with the resources necessary for membership. Organizational involvement in America has never been a random sample of the population, but in the early era of cyber-lobbying, the membership profile is less representative than one might have found among the physical participants in the union hall or community association.

**Differing Conceptions of Democracy.** Deliberation and opinion assessment offer two divergent views of democracy. The new technologies are more easily conceived of as tools for measuring the nature of opinion than as tools for supporting deliberation. "Deliberation entails debate, discussion, and persuasion in the public square." Using computer or interactive television technology to measure public support by "registering preferences on a keypad...falls short of democratic deliberation, in which participants' ideas rebound in the public sphere and are perhaps amended over time due to the weightier claims or more persuasive argument of a cohort voicing her concerns in the same public sphere."[17]

While there might be some intellectual appeal for direct democracy based on the *opinion assessment model*, most observers recognize that "uniformed or misinformed opinions can make terrible law, and yet the opinion of the majority is often exactly that."[18] While the speed and spread of the Web provides a powerful tool for informing individuals, lowering the entry costs for the formation of political groups and facilitating communications with decision makers, there is a danger in assuming that technology will erase the need for well-informed decision makers to filter and temper citizen demands. Pure democracy on the Web would be more likely to result in "rapid, often ill-considered political action...[and] can lead to government by whim. A single rumor on the Web, a sensational news story, or a well-organized campaign of misinformation might create a sweeping demand to do something that could turn out to be wrong, but be difficult or impossible to change."[19]

The ability of the public to immediately access information and communicate with leaders has been called the "tyranny of public opinion" in which "our leaders' ears are so close to the ground, they sometimes find it difficult to lead...the fatalistic perception that the American people are so plugged-in that it would be political suicide for leaders to stray away from popular opinion."[20]

While having political leaders serve as barometers of public opinion sounds democratic, such an approach has more validity when the issues are clear and simple and when the opinion is overwhelming. The process has less utility with complex issues and when there are deep and valid divisions.

President George W. Bush's agony over federal funding for stem cell research was played out under conditions where few members of the public understood the complexity of the issue and deep emotional conflicts cut across the public revealing untraditional cleavages. The president's progress in making the decision became a staple of news coverage for weeks. His highly publicized lecture from the Pope raised public awareness and the ante while giving some Catholic neutrals and undecided voters a new impetus for opposition. Public opinion polls indicating strong public support, at least among those who had not supported President Bush in the past, added to the controversy and raised important questions about how this decision would play out in terms of political strategy. Almost lost in the public debate was any expanded understanding of the issue itself. This decision is a key example of a situation where technology has provided "more citizen power with less citizen understanding."[21]

There is considerable fear that the *deliberative model* of democracy could be undermined by the capabilities of technology to deliver more information at a faster pace. "If politics is the art of negotiation, speed is the death of the political. Negotiation takes time...[and] negotiation and deliberate decisions become impossible. Speed privileges certainty and assertion....It is not possible to slow down long enough to allow time for uncertainty and questions."[22]

Requiring more of democracy than simply recording potentially poorly grounded preferences requires relatively open access to a wide variety of voices, allowing all ideas to be tested in the forge of open discussion. The "winners" in such battles over words are not necessarily based on who won in the past, or the loudness of the voices, but rather on the ability of the speakers to make their ideas compelling to a broad range of legitimate participants. As Anthony Wilhelm concludes, "While the Internet may be a potent medium for self-expression, it remains to be seen how effective it will be for collective action." Internet users often become "Awash in words and images in the absence of editing, filtering, and facilitation, not to mention [lack of support for]...virtues of listening to and cooperating with others."[23] Again, while it may not be inherent in the technology, our contemporary use of it favors opinion assessment rather than deliberation.

**Who Changes Whom?** The typical question has long been "How will technology change politics?" Hill and Hughes turn the question around, arguing that "the Internet is not going to radically change politics....As more and more people log on and participate in the Net's political forums, politics and society will change the Internet....Right now, politics in cyberspace is undoubtedly the playground of conservatives, libertarians and those with some kind of anti-government sentiment...[and] the Internet [did not make] these people conservative, libertarian or anti-government....[The Internet] merely attracted these groups of people because they feel that the government and the traditional media are not listening to them. The open, anarchic nature of the Internet naturally attracts the disaffected."[24]

Conservatives and libertarians also are more likely to have the resources and skills to use the emerging technologies. Hill and Hughes argue that "in the next few years, enough people will have access to the Internet to essentially dilute the political and demographic differences between the connected and unconnected."[25]

It is no surprise that liberals and Democrats, recognizing the political potential and their relative disadvantage, have been primary proponents of universal access to the Internet. In their attempt to even the playing field on the information superhighway (a recognizably dangerous place to play), they have pushed for wired schools, public information kiosks, computer literacy training, and a wide variety of other programs designed to reconfigure the demographics of the Internet.

In a broader context, the uses of technology are rooted in the traditional and normal operating procedures of the societies and institutions of which they are a part. Technologies may challenge or refine social organizations and traditions, but they seldom completely overwhelm them. In David Ronfeldt's view, "In the United States and other countries where democracy has deep roots, the information revolution may render up new instruments and opportunities for ordinary citizens to exercise their freedoms, improve their ways of life, make political choices, and protect their personal interests. But elsewhere, the tools of cyberdemocracy may give a state apparatus and its rules powerful new means of control over their citizenry, with an official ideology determining what information is allowed."[26]

Technologies are inserted into pre-established social and political contexts. There is a tug-of-war between the tendencies of the technology and the inertia of seemingly satisfactory forces of the status quo. When the character of a technology meshes with existing patterns, it can accelerate change. When the character of technology is at odds with the status quo, one or the other is forced to change.

**The Compromise for Representative Government.** Emerging information technology reduces the production and communication costs of information, while making geographic boundaries increasingly irrelevant.

Politicians in a representative democracy, rightfully concerned about their political base of supporters, have long made the distinction between the *quantity* and *quality* of the input they receive. Sheer quantity of input carries less weight than a quality communication that took considerable effort to produce, that provides important new information and that carries with it the subliminal message that the sender feels strongly enough to reevaluate his or her level of support for the recipient based on the recipient's response.

The very shrillness of conversation on the Internet, the ability of even the smallest and most unrepresentative group to broadcast its message, and the widespread publicity about hoaxes undermines Internet communications' credibility. As more individuals are exposed to flame wars and irrational attacks, there is a danger that public officials will begin to believe that the nets are populated only by such groups and that they can therefore ignore their pleas with impunity.[27]

Politicians increasingly operate under the principle that although cyberspace easily enables feedback to one's representatives, such feedback can reasonably be "devalued because of the sheer quantity and difficulty in processing it all. Great ideas and clear thinking stand even less of a chance in getting through the avalanche of cut-and-paste and add-your-name e-mail feedback...[and] if voluminous feedback replaces the judgment and character of representatives, then we have all of the disadvantages of a tyrannical democracy."[28] As more people turn to electronic communications, "the old-fashioned letter on paper, typed—or, better, laboriously hand-written—has, ironically, become more influential than the urgent screed on the screen."[29] The coin of the realm in politics is commitment more than simple communication. Elected officials use any clue they can get to assess quality communications that indicate a likelihood the sender will *act* on the basis of the issue raised.

Elected officials in America continue to be elected from geographic districts. "Unless they are planning to run for a higher office [and thus represent a larger geographic district], legislators couldn't care less about people who don't live in their districts. In fact, a flood of email and faxes from here, there and everywhere merely makes it harder for them to sort out how their own constituents feel."[30]

Elected officials turn to some of the same technologies to protect and promote their interests. Most members of Congress require potential e-mail senders to register their geographic address, allowing congressional staffs to sort out non-constituents. The ability to capture e-mail and snail-mail addresses electronically allows politicians an efficient way to create targeted mailing lists to broadcast the messages they wish to promote. Web sites of elected officials are less objective sources of unbiased information and more likely are used as promotional "bulletin boards," boosting political careers and/or preferred policy causes.

Few interest groups suggest e-mail as an effective way to communicate with elected officials. E-mail does serve as an effective way to communicate and strategize *among group supporters*, who are then encouraged to communicate using more traditional (but more respected) vehicles such as phone calls and personal letters. Groups increasingly use Web sites to capture the names of visitors who are likely prospects for membership.

The new technologies have largely been harnessed and tamed by existing power holders, with the impact largely on the margins rather than striking at the heart of standard operating procedures.

## Looking out for Yourself: Democracy R Us

Democratic governments are based on the principle of responsiveness to the needs and desires *of those who make their needs and desires known*. They are considerably less effective in anticipating unspoken needs. Just as democracy is not a spectator sport, it is also clear that it is unlikely that one will win if one does not play. Democracy, like nature, abhors a vacuum. It is seldom the case that if you don't participate no one will, but rather if *you* don't participate *someone else* will. Granting the playing field to others increases the likelihood that *their* preferences will trump yours.

## Residency: Think Nationally, Act Locally

There is little most of us can do about the societal and legal shifts which have torn us from communities of total commitment and temporarily planted us in communities of limited commitment. While a few of us might recognize the loss and change our lifestyles, it is impossible to go back since most of our neighbors will not have made the same decision. Being planted in a community of newcomers is not much different from being a peripatetic visitor in a geographically stable community. In either case there is little motivation or tendency to interact on anything more than a casual level.

If we cannot change our physical condition, we can change our attitude. Peripatetic lifestyles do not necessarily relegate us to political impotency. That is a decision, not a foreordained conclusion. With most of our neighbors moving as often as we do, fewer and fewer people have the right to lock out newcomers from the political process. Many communities are crying out for someone to step in and keep the political process vibrant.

There may even be a benefit to a constant influx of newcomers—*if* they become involved. They bring with them new ideas, new strategies and a potential new source of energy. Personal experience in other political jurisdictions, or information garnered from the Internet, often has direct applicability to the local condition. Virtual communities can help improve and enliven local communities to the degree that they stimulate action rather than increase lethargy. Politically active nomads will draw the attention of decision makers.

## Information: Resident versus Access

Information has always been a key power resource for the basic processes of politics: anticipating social problems, evaluating alternative solutions, and communicating with others in the hope of gaining their support.

In the age of scarce information and physically constrained limits on information discovery and communication, wisdom was likely to be recognized by one's *resident information*—the mastery of a known and relatively unchanging body of knowledge. Lawyers "read the law" at the feet of a master, who read much of the same law at the feet of his mentor. Diplomas hung on the walls of individuals, revealing their legitimacy as credentialed masters of law, medicine, philosophy or even political science. The sign of an intelligent person was the size of his or her library, since physical access to printed records was practically the only way to verify one's resident information or to build on it. Memory, recall and the creative formulation and application of information distinguished the mundane mimic from the master mind. While some updating was expected, it was largely an add-on to the basic body of knowledge.

The information revolution, in its various waves of technology, expanded the amount of information exponentially, increased the likelihood that new information would supercede old information and made physical access to printed documents less important. As the amount of information became greater than anyone could file away in their resident information memory and the availability of information was no longer limited to one's personal or local library, power shifted to those with greater *access information* skills. Increasingly, it is not so much what you can dredge up from your memory but rather what information you know how to *get* when needed that separates the informed from the less informed. Access information involves knowing where a piece of information exists, understanding the strengths and weaknesses of the information source discovered, and knowing how to apply it to a problem at hand. *Resident information* remains important to place newly discovered information into context, but learning in the modern world must be more of an ongoing process than it ever was in the past. Pasted on the basic skills of thoughtful inquiry and discovery is the need to evaluate and usually master new technologies of information access. While it is clear that the Internet and television contain some misinformation, the contemporary scholar or citizen who eschews their use does so at the peril of relegating one's information base to a lack of timeliness at a minimum and inadequacy in the long run.

If one hopes to engage in the political conversation, it behooves one to have information as current as one's fellow conversationalists (ideally even more current) and to seek out targets for one's conversation in the arena where they congregate. If the town square, political party clubhouse, newspaper editorial pages or seats around the cracker barrel are devoid of relevant fellow citizens, one could try to draw them back to their old haunts or, more likely, one might expend efforts finding out where they now congregate. That may be on line, or among local newcomer's clubs, social organizations or religious communities. One's current and relevant information can then become a tool for attracting interest and influencing behavior.

Honing one's access information skills is a constant process. It seems that just as we get comfortable with one set of tools, another comes along. We can either throw our hands up in frustration or glory in the human capacity to constantly improve on information access. The joy of living in a rapidly changing information environment is that we do not have to give up all our old tools. Even in the age of e-mail and e-books, it is still possible to write letters and curl up with a hard copy book.

## Where Does It All Leave Us?

In the most basic terms, *only* individuals can act politically. They may form groups or establish political organizations to magnify individual power, but it is still individuals who make choices and marshal the resources lent to them by others. You are, or at least you could be, one of those people.

Answers seldom come without well-framed questions. Questioning the present is the first step in understanding its nature and assessing the potential for change. The questions discussed in this book should get you thinking about your potential to make a difference politically, or at least give you some hints about why your level of participation is limited. The key lies in honestly applying the questions to your personal condition rather than thinking of them only in abstract terms. It is one thing to consider "Why do *they* act that way?" The potency of meaning increases when you ask, "Why do *I* act this way?"

All of the impediments associated with mobility and/or information processing can be overcome. Success is unlikely to lie in new technology or changes in mobility patterns. It emanates from within. As you look around at the players in the political process, most suffer under the same burdens you do. The difference lies in their implicit, or explicit, decisions, which allow them to rise above the obstacles.

If you have any needs that might be met by government and wish to address them, you must ask yourself four basic questions:

- Where do *I* live politically?
- What do *I* know?
- How do *I* know it?
- What am *I* going to do about it?

# Notes

## Chapter 1: The Where, What, How and So What of Politics

1. Abraham Lincoln, speech at Chicago, Illinois, July 10, 1858. Roy P. Basler (ed.), *The Collected Works of Abraham Lincoln*, New Brunswick, NJ: Rutgers University Press, 1953, Vol. 2, p. 498.

2. NBC, *Wall Street Journal* poll, of 2,011 adults, June 1999, LEXIS-NEXIS database.

3. Thomas Jefferson's letter to Colonel Charles Yancey, January 6, 1816. Suzy Platte, *Respectfully Quoted*, Washington, DC: Government Printing Office, 1989, p. 97.

4. Thomas Jefferson's letter to P. S. du Pont de Nemours, April 24, 1816. Suzy Platte, *Respectfully Quoted*, Washington, DC: Government Printing Office, 1989, p. 97.

5. Attributed to Edmund Burke, but never found in his formal writings. It may be a paraphrase of his view that "When bad men combine, the good must associate; else they will fall one by one, an unpitied sacrifice in a contemptible struggle." See Suzy Platte, *Respectfully Quoted*, Washington, DC: Government Printing Office, 1989, p.109.

6. For a series of stories of unlikely political activists, see Stephen Frantzich, *Citizen Democracy: Political Activists in a Cynical Age*, Lanham, MD: Rowman and Littlefield Publishers, 1999.

7. Inspired by a story told by Nicky Gumbel, Alpha series video.

## Chapter 2: Where Do You Live?

1. Robert D. Putnam, *Bowling Alone*, New York: Simon and Schuster, 2000.

2. Ibid., p. 35.

3. An October 1990 *Washington Post* poll of 1,004 adults found 25% claiming they were new to the community and could not register, while 3% did not know where to register. A 1996 *Los Angeles Times* poll of 1,426 pegged the figure for non-registrants "not having lived here long enough" at 22%. LEXIS-NEXIS database.

4. Steven J. Rosenstone and John Mark Hansen, *Mobilization, Participation and Democracy in America*, New York: Macmillan Publishing Company, 1993, p. 157.

5. John L. Locke, *The De-Voicing of Society*, New York: Simon and Schuster, 1998, p. 130.

6. See Peter Berger, *Invitation to Sociology*, New York: Doubleday Anchor, 1963, p. 49, and Robert Wuthnow, *Sharing the Journey*, New York: Free Press, 1994, pp. 5, 22.

7. Putnam, *Bowling Alone*, p. 204.

8. Current Population Surveys, reported by the Bureau of the Census., available at *http://www.census.gov/population/socdemo/migration/tab-a-txt*. Reported and analyzed in Claude S. Fisher, "Ever-More Rooted Americans," *http://ucdata.Berkeley.Edu/rsfcensus/papers/mobilitynov2000.pdf*.

9. Fisher, "Ever-more Rooted American,". p. 5.

10. January 2001 International Communications Research poll of 1,952 adults, LEXIS-NEXIS database; U.S. Census Bureau data available at *http://www.census.gov/population/socdemo/journey/ustime.txt*; and D'Vera Cohn and Katherine Shaver, "Commute Here among Worst," *Washington Post*, November 20, 2001, p. A4.

11. An October 1995 Gallup poll of 820 adults found that 25% of workers earning over $75,000 commute over 30 minutes compared to 16% of those with incomes from $15,000 to $29,000; 22% of low-income workers (less than $15,000 income), often having to rely on public transportation, reported a commute of over 30 minutes.

12. Long-term comparisons of physical mobility for specific population groupings is elusive. The pool of individuals in each educational grouping has changed

dramatically. In 1940 only about one-third of Americans had a high school diploma. By 1970, 70% of adults had graduated from high school. (Larry Long, *Migration and Residential Mobility in the United States*, New York: Russell Sage Foundation, 1988, p. 42).

13. U.S. Census Bureau, "Geographical Mobility," available at *http://www.census.gov/population/www/pop-profile/geomob.html.*

14. Recognizing both the impediments to voting and low participation levels, all of the military services aggressively encourage voting through voter assistance programs. Some data shows the military voting at higher levels than civilians after the introduction of these programs (see "Some See Military Vote Drive Aiding Commander in Chief," *Washington Post*, September 17, 1992, p. A8; see also press releases from the Federal Voting Assistance Program, Office of the Secretary of Defense). The closeness of the 2000 election and the extraordinary number of military voters in Florida led to a widespread discussion on the fairness of absentee ballot procedures and counting.

15. Sidney Verba and Norman Nie, *Participation in America*, New York: Random House, 1969, p. 247.

16. See Locke, *The De-Voicing of Society*, pp. 36–137.

17. Gary Jacobson, *The Politics of Congressional Elections*, New York: HarperCollins Publishers, 1992, p. 11.

18. Jacobson, *Politics*, p. 12.

19. David Butler and Bruce Cain, *Congressional Redistricting*, New York: Macmillan Publishing, 1992, p. 69.

20. Charles S. Bullock, "Affirmative Action Districts: In Whose Faces Will They Blow Up?" *Campaigns and Elections*, 1995 (April), p. 22.

21. A July 2001 *Washington Post* survey of 1,709 adults found that 86% of the public did not feel race should be used when drawing district lines. LEXIS-NEXIS database.

## Chapter 3: What Do You Need to Know? Requisites for Active Citizenship

1. For a more detailed discussion, see Stephen Frantzich, *Citizen Democracy*, Lanham, MD: Rowman and Littlefield, 1999, pp. 69–74.

2. John L. Locke, *The De-Voicing of Society*, New York: Simon and Schuster, 1998, pp. 119–120.

## Chapter 4: How Do You Know What You Know? The First Wave of Geography-Superceding Technologies

1. Within minutes of the attack, CBS producer Don Hewitt proposed sharing of all "generic video," and CBS president Andrew Heyward forged an agreement between all the networks. See Dana Calvo, "Networks Share Video in Rare Cooperation," *Los Angeles Times*, September 12, 2001, p. A1.

2. Although Marshall McLuhan never uses this phrase directly in his writings, the concept is heavily intertwined in his initial chapters of *Understanding Media: The Extensions of Man*, Cambridge, MA: MIT Press, 1994.

3. Precise figures on literacy in early America are difficult to come by. By the 1790s, 90% of men and 50% of women met the minimal standard of being able to sign their own wills, but this greatly overestimates functional literacy. See Kenneth Lockridge, *Literacy in Colonial America*, New York: W. W. Norton and Company, 1974, p. 39. In a clear understatement, Carl F. Kaestle (*Literacy in the United States*, New Haven, CT: Yale University Press, 1991, p. 54) points out that in early America, "the newspaper-reading public was far from universal." As late as 1850, only 3.3 papers were printed for each 100 citizens. By 1950 that figure reached its height of 35.3 and then declined to 20.7 by 1997 as individuals either ignored the news or sought other sources. Harold W. Stanley and Richard G. Niemi, *Vital Statistics on American Politics, 1999–2000*, Washington, DC: Congressional Quarterly Press, 2000, p. 167.

4. David Porush, "Ubiquitous Computing vs. Radical Privacy: A Reconstruction of the Future." *Computer-Mediated Communications Magazine,* March 1995 (*http://sunsite.unc.edu/cmc/mag/march*) .

5. See Douglas B. Craig, *Fireside Politics: Radio and Culture in the United States*, Baltimore and London: Johns Hopkins University Press, 2000, passim.

6. Cynthia J. Alexander and Leslie A. Pal (eds.), *Digital Democracy: Policy and Politics in a Wired World*, Toronto, Canada: Oxford University Press, 1998, p. 1.

7. Quoted in David Shenk, *Data Smog*, San Francisco, CA: HarperEdge, 1998, p. 60.

8. John P. Robinson and Geoffrey Godbey, *Time for Life: The Surprising Ways Americans Use Their Time*, University Park, PA: Pennsylvania State Press, 1997, p. 312.

9. Bruce M. Owen. *The Internet Challenge to Television*, Cambridge, MA: Harvard University Press, 1999, p. 19.

10. Nielsen ratings reported in the LEXIS-NEXIS database.

11. For a history of cable television and a detailed discussion of the development of C-SPAN, see Stephen Frantzich and John Sullivan, *The C-SPAN Revolution*, Norman, OK: University of Oklahoma Press, 1996, pp. 14–18.

12. Thomas Whiteside, "Onward and Upward with the Arts: Cable-2," *New Yorker*, May 27, 1985, p. 43.

13. Harold Stanley and Richard Niemi, *Vital Statistics on American Politics*, Washington, DC: Congressional Quarterly Press, 2000, p. 166. See also *The Index of Leading Cultural Indicators, 2001*, Washington, DC: Empower.org, 2001, p. 147, or available online at *http://www.empower.org*.

14. Ibid.

15. Shenk, *Data Smog*, p. 47.

16. Peter D'Agostino and David Tafler, *Transmission*, London: Sage Publications, 1995, p. 192.

17. Quoted in "The Battle (Zap! Click!) of the Sexes," *New York Times*, July 7, 1991, p. 122.

18. Empower.org, p. 146

19. Robinson and Godbey, *Time for Life,* p. 312.

20. John L. Locke, *The De-Voicing of Society,* New York: Simon and Schuster, 1998, p. 122.

21. See Robert Putnam, *Bowling Alone,* New York: Simon and Schuster, 2000, p. 217.

22. Mark Poster, "Cyberdemocracy," in David Holmes (ed.), *Virtual Politics: Identity and Community in Cyberspace,* London: Sage Publications, 1997, p. 217.

23. See S.B. Neuman, *Literacy in the Television Age: The Myth of the TV Effect,* Norwood, NJ: Ablex, 1991; and G.H. Brody, "Effects of Television Viewing on Family Interactions: An Observational Study," *Family Relations,* Vol. 29, April, 1990, pp. 216–220.

24. See Robert Kraut, et. al. "Internet Paradox: A Social Technology That Reduces Social Involvement and Psychological Well-Being?" *American Psychologist,* September 1998, p. 1021, available at
*http//www.spa.org/journals/amp/amp5391017.html*

25. Putnam, *Bowling Alone,* p. 218.

26. Ibid., p. 231.

27. Ibid., p. 237.

28. "Public Attentiveness to News Stories; 1986–2000." The Pew Research Center for the People and the Press, available at *http://people-press.org/database.htm*

# Chapter 5: How Do You Know What You Know? Computers, the Internet and Beyond

1. Robert Kraut et al., "Internet Paradox: A Social Technology That Reduces Social Involvement and Psychological Well-Being?" *American Psychologist,* September 1998, p. 1040, available at *http//www.spa.org/journals/amp/amp5391017.html*.

2. Bruce M. Owen, *The Internet Challenge to Television*, Cambridge, MA: Harvard University Press, 1999, pp. 10, 218.

3. In 1999, it was estimated that there were 4.9 million Web sites. A year later, the figure was estimated at 7.4 million. See *The Index of Leading Cultural Indicators 2001*, Washington, DC: Empower.org, p. 155.

4. David Shenk, *Data Smog*, San Francisco, CA: HarperEdge, 1998

5. Marshall McLuhan, *Understanding the Media: The Extensions of Man*, New York: McGraw-Hill, 1965, p. 358. This idea has been extended by Melvin Dubnick in "Educating Nomads: Narratives and the Future of Civic Education," paper presented at the 1998 Annual Meeting of the American Political Science Association. Available at *http://dubnick@mediaone.net*

6. Shenk, *Data Smog*, p. 75.

7. David Holmes, *Virtual Politics: Identity and Community in Cyberspace*, London: Sage Publications, 1997, p. 37.

8. Kevin A. Hill and John E. Hughes, *Cyberpolitics: Citizen Activism in the Age of the Internet*, Lanham, MD: Rowman and Littlefield Publishing Co., 1997, pp. 179–180, italics added.

9. John L. Locke, *The De-Voicing of Society*, New York: Simon and Schuster, 1998, p. 162.

10. Richard Davis, *Electronic Talk: Online Discussion and Public Opinion* (forthcoming).

11. Michael Margolis and David Resnick, *Politics as Usual: The Cyberspace "Revolution,"* Thousand Oaks, CA: Sage Publications, 2000, p. 209.

12. See Ronald J. Deibert, "Altered Worlds: Social Forces in the Hypermedia Environment," in Cynthia J. Alexander and Leslie A. Pal (eds.), *Digital Democracy: Policy and Politics in a Wired World*, Toronto, Canada: Oxford University Press, 1998, p. 40.

13. National survey of 3,184 adults conducted by the Pew Research Center for the People and the Press, "Internet News Audience Goes Ordinary," January 1999, available at *http://www.people-press.org/questionnaires/tech98que.htm*.

14. Alan Palmer, "Deleting Those Embarrassing Files...Completely," *Government Executive*, February 1991, p. 50.

15. See Jan Fernback and Brad Thompson, "Virtual Communities: Abort, Retry, Failure," paper presented at the May 1995 meeting of the International Communication Association, available online at
    *http//www.well.com/users/hlr/texts/VCivil.html*.

16. Cynthia J. Alexander and Leslie A. Pal (eds.), *Digital Democracy: Policy and Politics in a Wired World*, Toronto, Canada: Oxford University Press, 1998, p. 16.

17. *The Index of Leading Cultural Indicators, 2001*, Washington, DC: Empower.org, 2001, p. 155.

18. Shenk, *Data Smog*, p. 114.

19. Martin Heidegger, *The Question Concerning Technology and Other Essays*, New York: Harper and Row, 1977 [1952], p. 12.

20. Quoted in Shenk, *Data Smog*, p. 49.

21. Ibid., p. 88.

22. Anthony Wilhelm, *Democracy in the Digital Age*, New York: Routledge, 2000, p. 144.

23. See Michael Margolis and David Resnick, *Politics as Usual: The Cyberspace "Revolution,"* Thousand Oaks, CA: Sage Publications, 2000, p.113.

24. As indicated in Chapter 4, although McLuhan never used these specific words in his writings, it is a fair distillation of his ideas.

25. David Ronfeldt, "Cyberdomocracy Is Coming," *The Information Society Journal*, Vol. 8, No. 4, 1992, pp. 243–296. Available at: *www.cyberdomocracy.com/%21cyberoc.htm.*

26. Earl Shorris, quoted in Shenk, *Data Smog*, p. 125.

27. Quoted in John Markoff, "Portrait of a New, Lonelier Crowd Is Captured in an Internet Survey," *New York Times*, February 16, 2000, *http://content22a.nytimes.com/libr.../mo/biztech/articles/16online.html.* For the full report, see Norman Nie and Lutz Erbring, "Internet and Society," Stanford Institute for the Quantitative Study of Society, February 17, 2000, Available at *http://www.stanford.edu/group/siqss/Press_Release/Preliminary_Report-4-21.pdf.*

28. Nie and Erbring, "The Internet and Society."

29. Pew Research Center for the People and the Press, "Internet News Audience Goes Ordinary."

30. Kraut et al., "Internet Paradox," p. 1017.

31. David B. Whittle, *Cyberspace: The Human Dimension*, New York: W. H. Freeman and Company, 1997, p. 193.

32. J. McClellan," Netsurfers," *The Observer*, February 13, 1994, p. 10.

33. Locke, *The De-Voicing of Society*, p. 145.

34. Wayne Rash, Jr., *Politics on the Nets*, New York: W. H. Freeman, 1997, p. 171.

35. Hill and Hughes, *Cyberpoltics*, p. 72.

36. Pew Research Center for the People and the Press, "Internet News Audience Goes Ordinary."

37. Cass Susstein, *Republic.com,* Princeton, NJ : Princeton University Press, 2001, p. 59.

38. Andrew Chin, "Making the World-Wide Web Safe for Democracy," *Hastings Communications and Entertainment Law Journal*, #309, 1997, p. 328.

39. Shenk, *Data Smog*, p. 114.

40. Ibid., pp. 125–129.

41. Michele Wilson, "Community in the Abstract," in David Holmes (ed.), *Virtual Politics: Identity and Community in Cyberspace*, London: Sage Publications, 1997, p. 148.

42. Howard Rheingold, *Virtual Community: Homesteading on the Electronic Frontier*, Reading, MA: Addison-Wesley, 1993.

43. Pew Research Center for the People and the Press, "Internet News Audience Goes Ordinary."

44. Attributed to Amitai Etzioni on Web discussion groups.

45. See Stephen Frantzich, *Citizen Democracy: Political Activists in a Cynical Age*, Lanham, MD: Rowman and Littlefield Publishers, 1999, chapter 6.

46. Based on a list developed by Richard Parrish, "The Changing Nature of Community," paper presented at the 2001 annual meeting of the Midwest Political Science Association, p. 2.

47. Wilson, "Community in the Abstract," p. 148.

48. Pew Research Center for the People and the Press, "Internet News Audience Goes Ordinary."

49. Margolis and Resnick, "Politics as Usual," pp. 7, 26.

50. Kraut et al., "Internet Paradox," p. 1022.

51. Wilson, "Community in the Abstract," p. 153.

52. Rheingold, *Virtual Community*, p. 1.

53. See Fernback and Thompson, "Virtual Communities."

54. Rheingold, *Virtual Community*, p. 27.

55. Marshall Van Alstyne and Erik Brynjolfson, "Electronic Communities: Global Village of Cyberbalkans," paper presented at the 17th International Conference on Information Systems, December 1996, pp. 12, 17.

56. Anthony Wilhelm, *Democracy in the Digital Age,* New York: Routledge, 2000, p. 43.

57. Shenk, *Data Smog,* p. 111.

58. Fernback and Thompson, "Virtual Communities."

59. Parrish, "The Changing Nature of Community," p. 13.

60. Howard Fineman, "The Brave New World of Cybertribes," *Newsweek*, February 27, 1995.

61. Whittle, *Cyberspace,* p. 390.

62. Margolis and Resnick, *Politics as Usual,* p. 101.

63. Roger E. Levien, "The Civilizing Currency: Documents and Their Revolutionary Technologies," in Derek Leebaert (ed.), *Technology 2001: The Future of Computing and Communications*, Cambridge, MA: MIT Press, 1991, p. 210.

64. Ronfeldt, "Cyberdemocracy Is Coming."

# Chapter 6: What Do You Know? The Informed Citizen

1. See James Madison's letter to W. T. Berry, August 4, 1822, in *The Writings of James Madison*, Gaillard Hunt (ed.), New York: G. P. Putnam's Sons, 1910, vol. 9, p. 103.

2. See Jan Fernback and Brad Thompson, "Virtual Communities: Abort, Retry, Failure," paper presented at the May 1995 meeting of the International Communication Association, available on line at *http//www.well.com/users/hlr/texts/VCivil.html.*

3. Kevin A. Hill and John E. Hughes, *Cyberpolitics: Citizen Activist in the Age of the Internet*, Lanham, MD: Rowman and Littlefield Publishing, 1997, pp. 29–34. For

survey data on the demographics of Internet users, see the Pew Research Center for the People and the Press, available on the Web at *http://www.people-press.org*.

4. *The Index of Leading Cultural Indicators, 2001*, Washington, DC: Empower.org, 2001, p. 155, available at *http://www.empower.org*.

5. Michael Margolis and David Resnick, *Politics as Usual: The Cyberspace "Revolution,"* Thousand Oaks, CA: Sage Publications, 2000, p. 110.

6. Hill and Hughes, *Cyberpolitics*, pp. 29–34.

7. Ibid., pp. 35 and 43.

8. Felicity Barringer, "A Nation Challenged: The Rumor," *New York Times*, September 24, 2001, p. C9.

9. Howard Kurtz, "Peter Jennings, in the News for What He Didn't Say," *Washington Post*, September 24, 2001, p. C1. Also note that LEXIS-NEXIS searches underestimate the number of times a story is run since duplicate stories are deleted. News service stories run by a number of newspapers are only listed once. The number of stories reflect unique reporting by a newspaper or news service.

10. See "Media Learn an Amazing Fact: Reality," *Chicago Tribune*, February 12, 1992, p. 12.

11. See David Shenk, *Data Smog*, San Francisco, CA: HarperEdge, 1998, p. 160.

12. Based on a 1994 poll of adults carried out by the Network Television Association and the National Association of Broadcasters, reported in Harold Stanley and Richard Niemi, *Vital Statistics on American Politics, 1999–2000*, American Enterprise Institute: Washington, DC, 2000, p. 173.

13. Based on a December 1999 International Communications Research national survey of 1,506 adults. LESIS-NEXIS database.

14. Reinforcement arguments are made by individuals such as Cynthia J. Alexander and Leslie A. Pal (eds.), *Digital Democracy: Policy and Politics in a Wired*

*World*, Toronto, Canada: Oxford University Press, 1998; Bruce Bimber, "Toward an Empirical Mapping of Political Participation on the Internet, paper presented at the 1998 meeting of the American Political Science Association; Richard Davis, *The Web of Politics*, New York: Oxford University Press, 1999; B. Fisher, M. Margolis and D. Resnick, "Surveying the Internet: Democratic Theory and Civic Life in Cyberspace," *Southeastern Political Review*, Vol. 24, September 1996, pp. 399–429; Doris Graber, "The News Media and Politics: What Does the Future Hold?" *PS: Political Science and Politics*, Vol. 20, March 1996, pp. 33–36; R. P. Hiskes, "Acts of Democracy: Reconceptualizing Politics, Participation and Competence," *Public Perspective*, Vol. 7, No.4, June/July 1996, pp. 40–44.

15. For the empowerment argument, see Ted Becker and Christa Daryl Slaton, *The Future of Teledemocracy*, Westport, CT: Praeger, 2000; Howard Rheingold, *Virtual Community: Homesteading on the Electronic Frontier*, Reading, MA: Addison-Wesley, 1993; and Ed Schwartz, *Net Activism: How Citizens Use the Internet*, Sebastopol, CA: Songline Studios, 1996.

16. Robert Dahl, *Democracy and Its Critics*, New Haven: Yale University Press, 1989, p. 339.

17. Margolis and Resnick, *Politics as Usual*, p. vii.

18. Ibid., p. 208.

19. Alexander and Pal (eds.), *Digital Democracy*, p. 6.

20. David Croteau and William Hoynes, *By Invitation Only: How the Media Limit Political Debate*, Monroe, ME: Common Courage Press, 1994, p. 37.

21. See Rheingold, *Virtual Community*, p. 131; Michael Hauben, *The Netizen and the Wonderful World of the Net: An Anthology*, available at *http://www.columbia.edu/~hauben/netbook/1996*; and Wayne Rash, *Politics on the Nets: Wiring the Political Process*, New York: W. H. Freeman and Company, 1997.

22. Hill and Hughes, *Cyberpolitics*, p. 3.

23. Shenk, *Data Smog*, p. 137.

24. This is analogous to the alluring philosophy of the main character in the movie *Field of Dreams* who justifies building a major league stadium in an Iowa cornfield in order to draw back the great stars of the past.

25. Margolis and Resnick, *Politics as Usual*, p.109.

26. Based on polls by the Pew Research Center for the People and the Press, fall 2000 survey of 8,378 adult voters. Available at *http//www.people-press.org/questionnaires.online00que.htm*. The poll excludes the small percentage of adults (10%) relying solely the Internet for most of their news.

27. Margolis and Resnick, *Politics as Usual*, p. 114.

28. In economics, Gresham's Law asserts that cheap money drives out expensive money.

29. Pew Research Center for the People and the Press, national sample of 3,184 adults, December 1998. Available at *http//www.people-press.org/questionnaires/tech98que.htm*.

30. Shenk, *Data Smog*, pp. 15, 31, 124–125.

31. Margolis and Resnick, *Politics as Usual*, p. 212.

32. Schwartz, *Net Activism*, p. 158.

# Chapter 7: The Where, What and How of Politics in the Cyberdemocracy Age

1. See Peverill Squire, Raymond Wolfinger and David Glass, "Residential Mobility and Voter Turnout," *American Political Science Review*, Vol. 81, No. 1, March 1987, pp. 45–65; Roy A. Teixeira, *Why Americans Don't Vote*, New York: Greenwood Press, 1987, p. 74; and Steven J. Rosenstone and John Mark Hansen, *Mobilization, Participation and Democracy in America*, New York: Macmillan Publishing Company, 1993, pp. 158–159.

## NOTES

2. The data for this chapter come from the 2000 National Election Study (#3131) conducted by the Institute for Social Research at the University of Michigan. This national survey of eligible voters has become the standard for election research. In measuring that attention a respondent pays to various levels of campaigns (presidential or congressional) individuals were classified as "paying attention" if they reported paying "a great deal" or "quite a bit" of attention as opposed to "some," "very little," or "none." Further information on the survey is available from the ICPSR Web site at *http//www.icpsr.umch.edu*. All of the relationships reported are statistically significant. A statistically significant relationship is one that is very unlikely to happen by chance. For these relationships the chance is much less then 5 times out of 100 that such a pattern could develop randomly.

3. Rosenstone and Hansen, *Mobilization, Participant and Democracy*, pp. 157–158.

4. Ibid., p. 167.

5. See Howard R. Ernst, *The Housing Gap: A Political Analysis of American Voters by Housing Tenure*, University of Virginia, Center for Government Studies, 1999.

6. Ibid.

7. January 2001 International Communications Research poll of 1,952 adults, LEXIS-NEXIS database; U.S. Census Bureau data available at *http://www.census.gov/population/socdemo/journey/ustime.txt*; and D'Vera Cohn and Katherine Shaver, "Commute Here among Worst," *Washington Post*, November 20, 2001, p. A4.

8. Calculated by the author from the 2000 National Election Study (#3131) conducted by the Institute for Social Research at the University of Michigan. Pre- and post-election surveys represent views and demographics of the national adult population.

9. Peverill Squire, Raymond Wolfinger and David Glass, "Residential Mobility and Voter Turnout," *American Political Science Review*, Vol. 81, No. 1, March 1987, pp. 45–65.

10. Ed Schwartz, *Net Activism: How Citizens Use the Internet*, Sebastopol, CA: Songline Studios, 1996, p. 177.

11. David B. Whittle, *Cyberspace: The Human Dimension*, New York: W. H. Freeman, 1997, p. 396.

12. See Michael Margolis and David Resnick, *Politics as Usual: The Cyberspace "Revolution,"* Thousand Oaks, CA: Sage Publications, 2000, pp. 211–212.

13. Cynthia J. Alexander and Leslie A. Pal (eds.), *Digital Democracy: Policy and Politics in a Wired World*, Toronto, Canada: Oxford University Press, 1998, p. 1.

14. Theda Skocpal, "Associations without Members," *American Prospect*, July/August 1999, p. 66.

15. Ibid.

16. See Quenton Jones, "Virtual-Communities, Virtual Settlement and Cyber-Archeology: A Theoretical Outline," *Journal of Computer Mediated Communications*, December 1997, http://www.ascuc.org/jcmc/issue3/jones.html.

17. Anthony Wilhelm, *Democracy in the Digital Age,* New York: Routledge, 2000, p. 41.

18. Whittle, *Cyberspace*, p. 388.

19. Wayne Rash Jr., *Politics on the Nets*, New York: W. H. Freeman, 1997, pp. 170–171.

20. David Shenk, *Data Smog*, San Francisco, CA: HarperEdge, 1998, p. 135.

21. Ibid., p. 137.

22. Mark C. Taylor and Esa Saarinen, *Imagologies: Media Philosophy*, New York: Routledge, 1994, p. 6; see also, Wilhelm, *Democracy in the Digital Age*, pp. 6–7.

23. Wilhelm, *Democracy in the Digital Age*, p. 42.

24. Kevin A. Hill and John E. Hughes, *Cyberpolitics: Citizen Activism in the Age of the Internet*, Lanham, MD: Rowman and Littlefield Publishing, 1997, p. 182.

25. Ibid, p. 183.

26. David Ronfeldt, "Cyberdomocracy Is Coming," *The Information Society Journal*, Vol. 8, No. 4, 1992, pp. 243–296. Available at *http://www.cyberdemocracy.com/%21cyberoc.htm.*

27. Rash, *Politics on the Nets*, pp. 160–161.

28. Whittle, *Cyberspace*, p. 386.

29. Frances Cairncross, *The Death of Distance*, Boston, MA: Harvard Business School Press, 1997, p. 262.

30. Schwartz, *Net Activism*, pp. 122–123.

# Index

## A

AARP, 123
ABC, 98
Access information, 74, 131
Answering machines, 62, 80

## B

Berlin Wall, 44, 69
Bias, intentional, 66
Bias, structural, 66
Bookmarks, 84
Brynjolfson, Erik, 90
Bullock, Charles, 27
Burke, Edmund, 9
Bush, George H. W., 99
Bush, George W., 97–98, 125
Butler, David, 27

## C

Cable television, 44, 51–53, 71, 101
Cain, Bruce, 27
Cairncross, Frances, 121
Call waiting, 81–82
Caller ID, 80
Carpetbagger, 5
Challenger disaster, 57
Channel surfing, 53
Chat rooms, 87
Children's Defense Fund, 123
Cincinnatus, Lucius, 9
Clinton, Bill, 99
Clinton, Hillary, 5
CNN, 51–52, 75, 98
*Colgrove v. Green*, 26
Columbine High School, 57
Common Cause, 120
Communicating, 37–40, 53, 67, 80, 125
Communities; of interest; 25; of limited commitment, 15, 16, 59, 112, 130; of total commitment, 15, 16, 22, 59, 130
Community, 15, 22, 25, 29, 85–91
Commuting, 18, 19
Congress, U.S., 26, 36, 70, 97, 129
Constitution, 3
Conversation, 38, 81
Cookie, 77, 103

Couch potatoes, 52–53, 78
Croteau, David, 102
C-SPAN, 51, 75
Cyberdemocracy, 121

## D

Dahl, Robert, 101
Davis, Richard, 68
Declaration of Independence, 48
Democracy, 8, 9, 28, 30, 90, 92–93, 108, 122, 124–128, 131
Democrats, 27, 101, 127
Digital divide, 73

## E

Erbring, Lutz, 79
Education, 1, 64, 114–116, 118-120
Efficacy, 94
Election (2000), 57
E-mail, 24, 62, 69, 71, 75–77, 87, 97–98, 102, 128–129, 132; and anonymity, 65–66, 70–71, 86, 98
Empowerment and technology, 93, 101, 106
ESPN, 51
Etzioni, Amitai, 85

## F

*Federalist Papers*, 47
Fernback, Brad, 90
Flaming, 71, 98, 128
Founders, 3, 4
Fourteenth Amendment, 4, 26
Fragmentation (social/political), 57, 59, 78, 79, 89–90

## G

Geography, 3–7, 13, 14, 15, 16, 21, 22, 24, 26, 29, 68–70, 87–89, 109, 121, 129
Gergen, Kenneth, 15, 20
Government, 3
Gresham's Law, 104
Gun control, 34

## H

Hill, Kevin, 36, 67, 126
Home ownership, 112–113
House of Representatives, 4, 25
Hoynes, David, 102
Hughes, John, 36, 67, 126

## I

Ideology, 35
Income, 114–118, 120
Information, 64, 68, 72–74, 76-78, 82–85, 118, 127–120
Infotainment, 52
Interest groups, 123, 129, 133
Internet, 44, 62–69, 76, 79, 83–85, 87, 94–96, 101, 103, 125, 129, 132; and political participation, 68, 118–120; demographics, 67, 94–96, 103–104, 119–120
Islands of shared understanding, 37, 50
Isolation, 55–56, 82–83

## J

Jackson, Andrew, 48
Jennings, Peter, 98

## K

Keillor, Garrison, 21
Kennedy, John F., 50, 97
Kennedy, John-John, 44
King, Martin Luther, 44
Korean War, 48
Kraut, Robert, 61, 79, 88

## L

Lauden, Kenneth, 43
Lightner, Candy, 9, 32
Limbaugh, Rush, 98
Lincoln, Abraham, 5, 70
Locke, John L., 39, 43, 56

## M

Madison, James, 47, 93, 106
Margolis, Michael, 87, 91
McClellan, J., 80
McLuhan, Marshall, 45, 63, 75
Media, trust in, 100-101
*Miller v. Johnson*, 28
Mobility, 17, 18, 19, 20, 108–117
Mothers Against Drunk Drivers, 32
MSNBC, 102
MTV, 54
Municating, 40, 52, 65

## N

Narrowcasting, 37, 62
Newspapers, 47, 81, 99
Nie, Norman, 21, 79
Nixon, Richard, 44

North, Oliver, 71

## O

O'Neill, Thomas P., 28, 91
Onion peel theory, 97
Owen, Bruce, 62

## P

Parks, Rosa, 9
Paul, Richard, 13
Pentagon, 33, 45, 57
Political agenda, 31–33
Political participation, 13, 21–23, 56, 68, 108–120, 127–128; and education, 114–118; and home ownership, 109–118; and income, 114–118; and mobility, 109–118, 130–131
Political parties, 35, 112
Politics, 3
Poster, Mark, 56
Power, 31, 36
Problems, 33–34
Putnam, Robert, 14, 18, 55–57

## R

Radio, 48–50, 54, 62, 67, 92, 101, 122
Reagan, Ronald, 44
Redistricting, 26, 27
Remote control (TV), 53
Republicans, 27, 101
Resnick, David, 87, 91
Rheingold, Howard, 85, 89
Robbin, Jonathon, 74
Ronfeldt, David, 127
*Roots*, 51

## S

Sarnoff, David, 49
Schlesinger, Laura, 71
Schwartz, Ed, 106
Search engines, 73–74, 103
Seinfeld, Jerry, 54
Senate, 3, 5, 26
September 11 terrorist attack, 33, 43, 45–46, 97–98
Shenk, David, 63, 90, 103–105
Simpson, O. J., 57
Supreme Court, 26, 36
Susstein, Cass, 84

## T

Telephones, 80–82, 92, 94
Telephone tag, 81
Television, 49–57, 62, 79, 83; ratings, 50–51, 60; trust in, 100
Thall, Nelson, 75
Thompson, Brad, 90
Tocqueville, Alexis de, 122
Two-step flow of information, 47

## V

Values, 32, 34
Van Alstyne, Marshall, 90
VCR, 55
Verba, Sidney, 21
Viet Nam War, 48
Virtual communities, 6, 7, 24, 61, 85–91, 123, 131
Voter registration, 14
Voting, 111–120

## W

Web, 24, 62, 67, 71, 76–77, 84
Watson, Gregory, 9
Wilhelm, Anthony, 90, 126
Windows, 75
Word processing, 75
World Trade Center, 45, 57

Popular Politics
& Governance
In America

Steven Schier, General Editor

Popular Politics and Governance in America, a new series of books on contemporary political science, seeks to publish scholarly and teaching materials about the processes of popular politics and the operations of governmental institutions at both the national and state levels. Although many titles in this series will appeal to graduate and professional audiences, they will employ qualitative and quantitative analysis in fashions primarily appropriate for undergraduate classrooms. Topics will include studies of parties, interest groups, elections, public opinion, chief executives, legislatures, and the bureaucracy. Peter Lang views this new series as a flagship among their several on-going series that have published numerous well-received and useful volumes in political science.

For additional information about this series or for the submission of manuscripts, please contact:
Peter Lang Publishing, Inc.
275 Seventh Avenue, 28th floor
New York, New York 10001

To order other books in this series, please contact our Customer Service Department:
(800) 770-LANG (within the U.S.)
(212) 647-7706 (outside the U.S.)
(212) 647-7707 FAX

Or browse online by series:
www.peterlangusa.com